W9-CMS-435

WAYNE PUBLIC LIBRARY   MAY 1 5 2013

LARK JEWELRY & BEADING
beadweaving master class

JILL WISEMAN'S
BEAUTIFUL BEADED ROPES

LARK JEWELRY & BEADING
beadweaving master class

JILL WISEMAN'S
BEAUTIFUL BEADED ROPES
24 Wearable Jewelry Projects in Multiple Stitches

LARK CRAFTS
Asheville

Editor
Nathalie Mornu

Technical Editor
Judith Durant

Editorial Assistance
Dawn Dillingham
Hannah Doyle
Abby Haffelt

Art Director
Kathleen Holmes

Production
Jackie Kerr

Illustrator
Melissa Grakowsky

Photographer
Lynne Harty

Cover Designer
Kay Holmes Stafford

LARK CRAFTS
An Imprint of Sterling Publishing
387 Park Avenue South
New York, NY 10016

If you have questions or comments about
this book, please visit: larkcrafts.com

Library of Congress Cataloging-in-Publication Data

Wiseman, Jill.
  Jill Wiseman's beautiful beaded ropes : 24 wearable jewelry projects in multiple stitches. – First Edition.
    pages cm
  ISBN 978-1-4547-0356-3 (hardback)
  1. Beadwork--Patterns. 2. Jewelry making. I. Title.
  TT860.W597 2012
  745.594'2--dc23

                              2012002269

10 9 8 7 6 5 4 3 2 1

First Edition

Published by Lark Crafts
An Imprint of Sterling Publishing Co., Inc.
387 Park Avenue South, New York, NY 10016

Text © 2012, Jill Wiseman
Photography © 2012, Lark Crafts, an Imprint of Sterling Publishing Co., Inc., unless otherwise specified
Illustrations © 2012, Lark Crafts, an Imprint of Sterling Publishing Co., Inc.

Distributed in Canada by Sterling Publishing,
c/o Canadian Manda Group, 165 Dufferin Street
Toronto, Ontario, Canada M6K 3H6

Distributed in the United Kingdom by GMC Distribution Services,
Castle Place, 166 High Street, Lewes, East Sussex, England BN7 1XU

Distributed in Australia by Capricorn Link (Australia) Pty Ltd.,
P.O. Box 704, Windsor, NSW 2756 Australia

The written instructions, photographs, designs, patterns, and projects in this volume are intended for the personal use of the reader and may be reproduced for that purpose only. Any other use, especially commercial use, is forbidden under law without written permission of the copyright holder.

Every effort has been made to ensure that all the information in this book is accurate. However, due to differing conditions, tools, and individual skills, the publisher cannot be responsible for any injuries, losses, and other damages that may result from the use of the information in this book.

Manufactured in China

All rights reserved

ISBN 13: 978-1-4547-0356-3

For information about custom editions, special sales, and premium and corporate purchases, please contact the Sterling Special Sales Department at 800-805-5489 or specialsales@sterlingpub.com.

Submit requests for information about desk and examination copies available to college and university professors to academic@larkbooks.com. Our complete policy can be found at www.larkcrafts.com.

6

CONTENTS

102

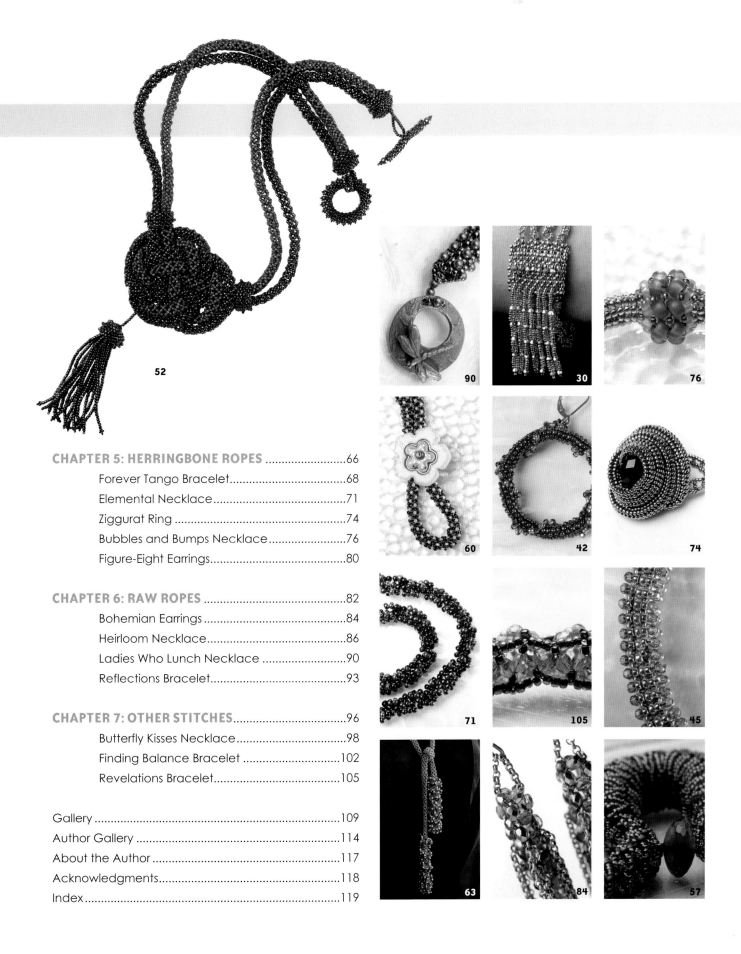

INTRODUCTION

When I was young, I wanted to grow up to be an author. Of course, at that time the vision included moving to a lovely cottage in the English countryside to write romance novels, and a brooding, handsome man named Drake. Instead I got stuck with the super-heated summers of Texas and a dog named Winston. But I think I got the better deal anyway, since writing this book allows me to share my beaded rope jewelry for you to create, wear, and enjoy.

You'd think defining a beaded rope would be fairly straightforward. But when I polled fellow beaders, I discovered it isn't. Should a rope be round with a hollow center? Some think a rope must have a solid core. Can something square or triangular be considered a rope? Can earrings be long enough to be considered ropes? How thick can something become before it's no longer a rope?

Playing with all these questions, I created my own interpretations of the many suggested incarnations of beaded ropes. I use a single bead core in the Butterfly Kisses Necklace, for example, and make a triangular rope in the Reflections Bracelet. For Josephine's Fortune Necklace and the Forever Tango Bracelet, I manipulate the rope into different shapes—a knot, and a sort of lasso. The beadwork in the Abundance Necklace goes thin to really thick and back again. And while the Bohemian Earrings may be short, they look graceful thanks to the addition of delicate chains, and they definitely count as ropes! As you'll find in the last chapter, sometimes a rope can hold an element of surprise. The Finding Balance Bracelet looks like it's made of peyote stitch, but it's actually brick stitch with the peyote beads added directly on the band. In all these designs I stay true to my personal design creed, creating pieces you won't find intimidating to make and will wear in your daily life.

Each chapter in this book explores a different stitch. Starting with the versatile spiral rope stitch, I include a variety of looks to show how the choice of material and minor adjustments—like how many beads you include in a loop—

can produce dramatically different results. Peyote ropes are common, but why settle for plain when you can embellish them so easily and in so many ways, leading to a richer design? The incredible flexibility of netted ropes leads to a myriad of ways to direct and arrange them into patterns and knots. Likewise, herringbone ropes are shown in ways you may not have imagined before, as in the Ziggurat Ring. Right angle weave ropes offer a structure that begs to be elaborated upon with color and pearls and sparkly beads.

So come discover the possibilities of beaded ropes. Drake, Winston, and I wish you lots of fun!

CHAPTER 1
SUPPLIES AND TECHNIQUES

Most beadweavers work with a very similar bag of tricks, which includes

beads, thread, and other tools, as well as a variety of stitches, such as peyote,

herringbone, right angle weave, and so on. And we all have our own ways of

manipulating these materials and techniques. Here are my methods.

Beads

It all starts with the shiny things. Color, size, shape, sparkle—these are the things that first attract us; once we discover all the things we can do with beads, there's no end to the love affair. Here are some of my favorites.

Round Seed Beads

Seed beads are the food for my soul. My general feeling is the smaller the better, but strangely, not everyone agrees with me on that! (Darn those aging eyes.) Seed beads are primarily manufactured in Japan and the Czech Republic, although we're starting to see them coming from China as well. I find the quality of seed beads from China to be so irregular as to be unusable, so I stay away from them. Japanese seed beads have the most consistent sizing and biggest holes, so they're a mainstay of my work. I also love the unique colors and slightly smaller sizing of the Czech seed beads, so I keep a good supply of them on hand as well.

As a general rule, among the Japanese manufacturers, Matsuno and Toho create a wider seed bead, while Miyuki beads are narrower. Czech seed beads have smaller holes and can be overall smaller in size than the Japanese beads, even though they're both referred to as the same size.

Seed beads come in many different sizes. The larger the number, the smaller the bead. For beadweaving purposes, size 6° is generally the largest size used, with size 15° being the smallest. Size 11° is the most commonly used and has the greatest variety of colors available.

You can find one-cut, two-cut, and three-cut seed beads in both Czech and Japanese brands. A cut is a facet sliced off the side of a seed bead, creating a spot for the light to flash off as the bead moves. These are also sometimes referred to as charlottes.

Tip: It's useful to have a bead stash with a large variety of bead sizes, colors, and types. Having the same color bead in

several different sizes is also great so you can always coordinate color schemes the way you'd like.

Cylinder Beads

Cylinder beads are tubular beads made by the Japanese manufacturers Miyuki and Toho. They're usually referred to by their brand names: Delicas, Treasures, or Aikos. Although you'll find 11°s to be the size most people use, they now come in a range of other sizes: 8°, 10°, and 15°. They fit together very precisely and can create a strong fabric with no space showing between the beads. Because of the cylindrical shape, these are best reserved for projects that require flatwork or squared-off ends. They don't usually work well in pieces that are curved.

Crystals

If you love sparkle, then crystals are your friends! I primarily use Swarovski crystals from Austria for their high lead content, large holes, and consistent quality. Swarovski also makes my beloved tiny 2-mm round crystals, which are just a

wee bit larger than an 11° seed bead. This makes them perfect for use in beadweaving projects, although you do have to be careful that they don't cut the thread with their sharp edges.

Fire-Polished Beads

These faceted oval beads come from the Czech Republic and offer sparkle of their own with a lower price tag than crystals. The facets aren't as sharp because they don't have the high lead content of crystals, but they still manage to pack a great deal of shine.

Lampwork/Focal Beads

I'm a huge admirer and collector of handmade glass beads, or lampwork beads, made one at a time by glassworkers who melt rods of glass in the flame of a torch and magically create little works of art. Lampwork beads are wonderful as focal components in beadweaving pieces. Other focal bead options include large gemstones, polymer clay, ceramic, and raku.

Clasps and Findings

Sometimes I use beadwoven clasps on my pieces, and other times I use special clasps I've found during my beady travels. In this book, most of the pre-made clasps are artisan created instead of mass produced. I also enjoy adding materials that are not often seen in beadweaving. For example, I included chain in the Bohemian Earrings. You can find chain in all sorts of different sizes and finishes, which allows for many designing options.

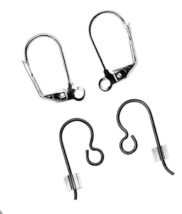

Tools and Materials

There are many different threads, needles, and other tools available to beadweavers, and we all have our favorites for a variety of personal reasons. Here's what I choose.

Thread

My first thread choice is FireLine because I like the strength, the availability of multiple weights (diameters), and the fact that it's waterproof. My second choice is WildFire, for the same reasons, but it's a bit thicker than my usual 6 lb. FireLine, which makes it unsuitable for projects that require multiple passes through small bead holes. I rarely use nylon thread unless I need a particular color for a design element. If I do use nylon thread I turn to C-Lon because I like the drape and feel of it. Try all the threads available until you find your favorites. There's no right or wrong answer here, only preference. However, I would urge you to use a braided beading thread/fishing line like FireLine when you're working with crystals because it stands up better over time to the cutting action of sharp crystal edges.

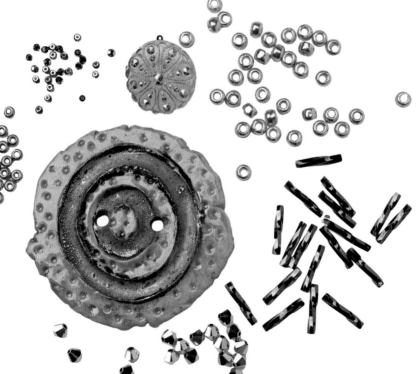

Thread Conditioners

I rarely use any type of thread conditioner, but if my FireLine acts up and gets all tangled, I sometimes run microcrystalline wax over it. I no longer use beeswax as a conditioner because I dislike its stickiness. The other option is Thread Heaven, which I will also use if it's what's available.

Needles

My needle of choice is a size 11 Tulip needle. This size and brand gets me through 95% of my beading without having to change to a smaller size. You can use a size 11 needle as a substitute for a size 10 or 12 in any of the projects in this book. I like the Tulip brand because the needle is flexible but doesn't become bent as I use it, the way other brands do. I also keep on hand size 10, 12, and 13 long beading needles from either John James or Pony, as well as some small Sharps (short) needles for the rare times I need them to turn an extreme corner.

Scissors

I use inexpensive thread clippers so that when the blade dulls, I won't hesitate to toss them out and get a new pair. Having a sharp blade allows you to make a precise cut very close to the beads to keep your thread from showing.

Dowels

Many beadweavers find it difficult to bead tubular work like the beaded ropes in this book without having some sort of cylindrical form or dowel in the center of the tube. If this makes it easier for you, by all means use one. You can find round dowels in various sizes at home improvement or craft stores, and you can also be inventive by using a pencil, bead tube, or any other tubular object you have at home if the diameter is appropriate for your project.

Beading Surfaces

The most common beading surface is a mat made of Vellux, either cut from a blanket or purchased at your local bead store. Because I always have multiple projects going on at the same time, I like to work in jewelry trays. Mats with different types of surfaces are available as insets for the trays—I use light-colored velvet. The benefit of trays for me is that they can be easily moved around and stacked as I switch from one project to another.

Other Tools

There are a bunch of other tools I like to use; they're nice to have but not required.

Bobbins are small plastic cases to wind your thread around and keep it from tangling.

Chain-nose pliers can be used to pull a needle through a tight bead, but be careful—you could break the bead!

An **awl** will help pick out knots in your thread.

Use a **task light** for extra illumination, especially when traveling or taking bead classes.

Use a **bead scoop** or **triangle** to help pick up beads from your mat and return them to the bead container.

Calipers will measure a bead if the size isn't marked.

A **needle case** will keep you organized.

Tape measures help ensure pieces will fit the way you like them.

Basic Beading Tips

Before we get into the nitty-gritty of specific stitches, here are a few guidelines that apply to all of your beadweaving, no matter the stitch.

Single Thread versus Doubled Thread

I always use a single thread. Always. If I try to switch it up and use a doubled thread I invariably get into a heap of trouble when I try to back out of a bead or two. If I'm in doubt about the sturdiness of my thread, I either use a heavier weight of FireLine or I stitch everything twice to get that second pass of thread. Yup, really.

Precision

I love the look of perfectly precise beadwork, and that usually means not taking a lot of shortcuts. Don't get me wrong—if there's a way to make it quicker and easier without affecting the look of the finished product, I'm all for it! But if you can see where beads aren't sitting just right, or if the piece is pulling awkwardly, that dampens my enjoyment.

Which means I make my herringbone stitches with only two beads at a time, not four beads at a time as I've seen others do. And when I do right angle weave (RAW),

I stitch through one bead at a time and pull for tension after each stitch instead of scooping through multiple beads. Each bead is going in a different direction, and if you tighten in that direction it makes a big difference in how the bead sits.

Tension

One of the most common problems is difficulty keeping good tension. While some people actually bead with very tight tension, most people bead loosely and this shows up as limp projects with visible thread. Here are a few tips to help bead with an even, firm tension.

- As you hold the piece in your hands, lightly pinch the spot where the thread is exiting the beads, rather than letting the thread slip between stitches. This holds the tension. But don't stress your hands by pinching hard all the time! Just a light hold is enough.

- As you pull the thread through the beads in a stitch, place your thumb and forefinger over the spot the thread is moving through. This keeps the beads from pulling away from the piece in response to the thread movement.

- After each stitch, take an extra little tug on the thread to help tighten it up. Be sure to tighten in the direction the thread is exiting the bead. If it's exiting in a north direction, for example, you should pull to the north.

- Using beeswax as a thread conditioner can give your thread a little extra grip.

Culling Beads

The more uniform your bead sizes are, the better the finished piece will be, so don't be afraid to cull out overly wide or extra skinny beads. It's okay to be picky! I have a clear vase in my home where I put all the culled beads so they still get to be used as art.

Adding and Ending Threads

When I start working, I leave a tail of 4 to 6 inches (10.2 to 15.2 cm) to weave in later, as follows.

With the tight weave of peyote stitch I don't tie any knots as I'm adding or ending off threads. Instead, I simply weave through several beads on a diagonal, changing directions at least three times, and I work in a figure-eight pattern so the thread crosses back over itself at least once.

For all other beadweaving stitches I do a combination of weaving through the beads and tying a few half-hitch knots along the way. When tying a half-hitch knot (figure 1 shows you how), if you pull your thread down so you have a very small loop before you go through it, the knot is less likely to tighten prematurely, causing you to have to pick it out.

figure 1

14

The Stitches

The projects in this book require the following techniques.

Spiral Rope

For this example we'll use size 8° and 11° seed beads, where the 8's form the core or spine and the 11's form the spiral loops. String three 8's and four 11's, leaving about 6 inches (15.2 cm) of thread below them. Pass again through the 8's only from the tail end back up to the top (figure 2).

To continue adding loops, pick up one 8° and four 11's. Pass through the last three 8's added, and push the loop to the right (figure 3). Repeat until you reach the desired length.

When adding or ending thread in a spiral rope, I always tie my half-hitch knots in the loops rather than along the center core because I don't want to block my access to weaving through the core beads again later.

figure 2

figure 3

The beauty of a spiral rope is the infinite number of variations you can create. You can use 6's, 8's, or 11's as the center core beads. You can make short tight loops with fewer beads or long floppy ones using more beads. You can add accent beads such as 3-mm fire-polished beads or drop beads in the loops. Your imagination is your only limit.

Tubular Peyote Stitch

As a right-hander, I work around to the left so I can see where I'm going. Lefties will work in the opposite direction, but everything else is the same. If you find you're working in a direction that feels uncomfortable, at the end of a round after you step up you can tie a half-hitch knot and then pass through the nearest up bead (in case you don't know what they are, "up beads" are defined in Round 4) to change direction.

Rounds 1 and 2 String an even number of beads and leave a 4- to 6-inch (10.2 to 15.2 cm) tail below them. Pass through all the beads again to form a ring, and then move forward one bead so the working thread exits the same bead out of which the tail thread is coming.

Round 3 String one bead, skip one bead, and then pass through the next bead; repeat to the end of the round. At the end of each round you'll need to step up to get in position for the next round. Here you'll pass through the first bead added in the current round (figure 4). The beads in this round will sit off to the side instead of up into a tube, but that will get fixed in the next round.

Round 4 From here on you'll see that the beads alternate between those that stick out (called up beads) and those that are recessed (called down beads). String one bead and pass through the next up bead in the round. Repeat to the end of the round, and then step up through the first bead added in the current round (figure 5). Make sure you're pulling the thread tightly to help the beads sit upward and form a tube.

Repeat Round 4 until you have the desired length.

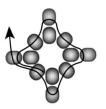

figure 4

figure 5

Flat Peyote Stitch

Flat peyote stitch is worked the same as tubular, but you work back and forth in rows rather than around in circles. Joining two pieces or the beginning and ending rows is called zipping. One of the edges has to have an up bead as its first bead, and the other edge has to have a down bead as the first bead. Pass through an up bead on one edge, then an up bead on the other edge, repeating across the rows to zip the whole length of the edges together.

Tubular Netting with Step Up

For this example we'll assume two bead colors, A (white) and B (pink).

1 String one A and one B; repeat five more times for a total of 12 beads. Move them down the thread, leaving a 6-inch (15.2 cm) tail. Starting from the tail end, pass through all the beads again to form a ring, and then move forward one more bead to exit an A bead (figure 6).

2 Pick up one B, one A, and one B. Skip three beads on the ring and pass through the fourth bead, an A bead (figure 7). Repeat twice to form three wings. On the first round, your wings will sit off to the side of the base circle. Don't worry about this because you'll coax them to sit up on the next round by using tight tension.

3 After completing the last wing of each round, step up by passing through the first two beads added in the round (figure 8). The thread exits the middle bead of a wing.

4 Pick up one B, one A, and one B. Pass through the middle bead of the next wing, an A bead (figure 9). Repeat twice to form three wings and step up. Repeat adding rounds until you've reached the desired length.

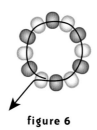

figure 6

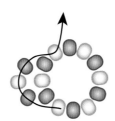

figure 7

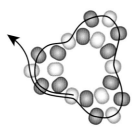

figure 8

figure 9

You can make variations of tubular netting by using more beads in your wings for a more open-weave look, by experimenting with color placement, or by using different kinds of beads such as fire-polished or drop beads.

Tubular Netting with No Step Up

Once again, we'll use two colors for the example, A (white) and B (teal).

1 String one A and one B. Repeat six more times for a total of 14 beads. Move them down the thread, leaving a 6-inch (15.2 cm) tail below. Starting from the tail end, pass through all the beads again to form a ring, and then move forward one more bead past the tail, exiting an A bead.

2 String one B, one A, and one B. Skip three beads in the ring and pass through the fourth bead, an A. Repeat twice to form three wings. String one B, one A, and one B and then pass through the middle bead of the first wing (figure 10). It seems like it's a huge jump for that last stitch, but it's correct.

3 Continue stringing one B, one A, and one B and then passing through the middle bead of the next wing until you've reached the desired length.

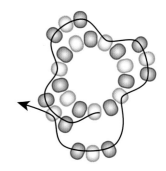

figure 10

Tubular Herringbone Stitch

Tubular herringbone stitch begins, and sometimes ends, with ladder stitch, which is outlined below in steps 1 through 6.

1 String on four beads and push them down, leaving about a 6-inch (15.2 cm) tail. From the tail end moving back upward, pass through the first two beads (figure 11).

2 The beads that were on top will fold over so that you have two beads next to two beads. You might have to nudge the beads to make them fold over the way they should. Without adding any beads, pass from top to bottom through the two beads on the right so you're at the end of the four-bead section and ready to add more beads (figure 12).

3 Pick up two beads and pass from top to bottom through the beads on the left (figure 13). You're anchoring the beads you just picked up to the rest of the section.

4 Now you need to get to the end of the section again to be able to add more beads, so without adding any more beads, pass from bottom to top through the two beads to the right (figure 14).

5 Continue adding two beads at a time until you have a group eight beads wide by two beads tall.

Tip: Remember that when you add two beads, you need to anchor them to the bead strip by passing through the beads in the opposite side from where the working thread is exiting. Then you have to get to the end of the strip to be in position to add more beads by passing through the beads you just added.

figure 11

figure 12

figure 13

figure 14

6 Fold the strip in half like a taco. Pass through the beads on both ends in a circle to join them, and end by coming out the top of any bead (figure 15).

Finally—now we get to start with herringbone stitch! You'll pick up two beads at a time, and as you work you'll notice the beads will tilt toward each other instead of sitting up straight. This is exactly what you want. That's what makes the herringbone V pattern. You'll also notice that you're going to end up with four vertical columns that seem like they're not attached to each other. Don't worry—they are attached, but it's low in the stitch, so it looks like columns as you're working. At the end you'll bring the columns together so there's no separation.

7 Pick up two beads and pass through the first bead on the left (from top to bottom), then through the next bead to the left (from bottom to top) to get in a position to add more beads (figure 16). You may need to nudge one of the beads you just added to get it to sit in place. Repeat three times.

figure 15

figure 16

8 After adding the last set of beads in the round you'll need to step up to be in position to start the next round. So for the very last pass you'll go through two beads to come out the top (figure 17).

9 Repeat steps 7 and 8 until you reach the desired length.

10 After you've completed the last round, connect the last two beads of each vertical column to each other by circling around them, following the same thread path used for ladder stitch at the beginning (figure 18).

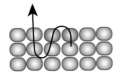

figure 17

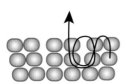

figure 18

Tubular Right Angle Weave

Right angle weave is commonly known as RAW. Let's begin with a terminology lesson. Each RAW unit has four sides and I refer to them here as follows (figure 19).

- The top of the unit is the "roof."

- The bottom of the unit is the "floor."

- The right side of the unit is the "right wall."

- The left side of the unit is the "left wall."

These instructions show units that have two beads per side, but you can work RAW with as many beads per side as you need or want.

Roof

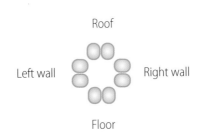

Left wall — Right wall

Floor

figure 19

One of the rules of RAW is that your thread should never cross straight through an intersection. Here's what I mean by that. Figure 20 shows the thread crossing the intersections (wrong), but figure 21 shows how the thread path should look when finished (correct).

Another rule is that you alternate clockwise and counterclockwise thread paths between units. This requires some extra passing through beads to get where you want to go without the thread crossing intersections. This is normal—don't feel like you're doing something wrong.

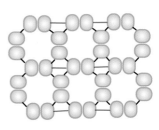

figure 20

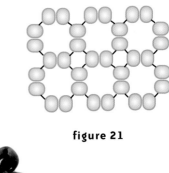

figure 21

18

1 Pick up eight beads and push them down, leaving about a 6-inch (15.2 cm) tail. Working from the tail end back up, pass through all eight beads again to form a ring, and then go through the first two beads one more time (figure 22).

If you use your imagination, the ring will look like figure 23.

2 Pass through the two beads that form the roof, and then down through the two beads that form the right wall (figure 24).

3 Pick up six beads and anchor the new beads by passing again through the two beads that form the right wall of the first unit (figure 25). As you add each new unit, you'll alternate passing clockwise and counterclockwise through the beads that form the right wall.

4 Pass through the two floor beads of the new unit, and then up through the two right wall beads to get to the outside edge so you can add more beads (figure 26).

5 Continue adding units in this manner until you've reached the desired length.

6 To start a new row, pass through the beadwork so the thread exits the roof beads of the last unit.

If the thread in the last unit was exiting down, then the thread moves in a clockwise direction to exit the roof beads (figure 27). If the thread in the last unit was exiting up, then the thread moves in a counterclockwise direction to exit the roof beads (figure 28).

figure 22

figure 23

figure 24

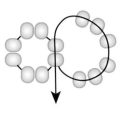

figure 25

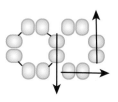

figure 26

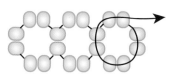

figure 27

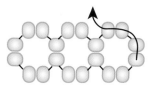

figure 28

At this point I like to flip my work over so I can continue working from left to right. Because I'm right-handed, this allows me to see the beads I'm working on with the least awkward hand position.

7 String six beads for the first unit of the next row. If the thread was moving in a clockwise direction on the last unit and the thread is exiting to the outside of the piece, then you'll work in a counterclockwise direction to attach these new beads. (If it wasn't going in a clockwise direction, skip to the next paragraph.) Pass through the two beads originally exited, all six of the beads added, and through the next two roof beads of the previous row (figure 29), then go on to step 8.

If the thread was moving in a counter-clockwise direction on the last unit and the thread is exiting to the inside of the piece, then you'll work in a clockwise direction to add the new beads. Pass through the two beads originally exited, and the two beads on the left wall of the current unit (figure 30), then continue to step 9.

For the remaining units of each row, you'll only have to pick up four beads, because two of your unit sides are already there (the floor and the left wall).

8 String four beads and pass through the left wall of the previous unit, the floor of this unit (which is the roof of the unit from the previous row), and the first two beads strung (figure 31).

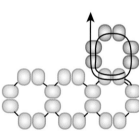

figure 29

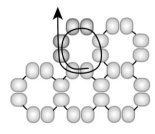

figure 30

figure 31

9 String four beads and pass through the floor of this unit (which is the roof of the unit from the previous row), the left wall beads of the previous unit (which is the right wall of this unit), the four beads just strung, and the roof beads of the next unit from the previous row (figure 32).

Alternate steps 8 and 9 until you've finished the row. To start the next row, work steps 6 and 7, then alternate steps 8 and 9 for the remainder of the row.

10 On the last row you'll join the long edges together to create a tube as follows. String two beads and pass through the two edge beads on the opposite side of the piece; string two beads and pass

through the original beads exited, then move into position to add the next two beads (figure 33). The thread paths will mirror those used in adding new units as shown in steps 8 and 9.

Now it's on to the projects. I encourage you to play with these designs and make them your own. They can be scaled up in size by using larger beads (size 8° in place of size 11°, for instance) or scaled down by exchanging smaller beads. Instead of using all sparkly crystals, what would happen if you used matte beads in their place? Consider these projects to be a jumping-off place to spark your own creativity!

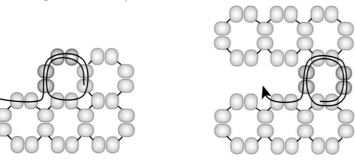

figure 32   **figure 33**

CHAPTER 2
SPIRAL ROPES

DEW DROP
SPIRAL NECKLACE

This project is an unusual variation of a spiral rope—peyote stitch

embellishes each loop to create a textured spiral. You can make a

bracelet or a necklace simply by making the rope shorter or longer.

► Bead Loop One

1 Using a comfortable length of thread, string five 8°s and nine As; push them down the thread so there's 6 inches (15.2 cm) of tail below them. Pass back up through the 8°s and the first A (figure 1).

2 Flip the work over so the tail thread is at the top. Peyote stitch along the length of As in the loop with Bs (figure 2).

3 When you get to the end, flip the work so the tail is at the bottom again, and then pass through the five 8° spine beads to exit from the top of the column.

► Add Loops

1 String one 8° and nine As. Pass through the top five 8° spine beads and the first A. Flip the work over and peyote stitch along the length of As in the loop with Bs. Flip the work and pass back through the top five spine beads only.

2 Add one new 8° spine bead to the top every time you add a new loop of 11°s; secure it by passing through only the top five 8° spine beads, including the one you just added.

figure 1

figure 2

TIP

Make sure you don't hook your thread on the beads as you work. I like to hold my hand over the area I'm working, exposing just a small section of the rope, and use my hand as a shield to keep the thread from catching.

SUPPLIES

Size 8° russet rose permanent galvanized round seed beads, 0.33 gram per inch (2.5 cm) of rope

Size 11° round seed beads

> **Color A: amber/dark cranberry lined, 1 gram per inch (2.5 cm) of rope**

> **Color B: russet rose permanent galvanized, 0.5 gram per inch (2.5 cm) of rope**

1-inch (2.5 cm) toggle clasp

Size 10 or 12 beading needles

Beading thread

Beading mat

Scissors

FINISHED SIZE

21 inches (53.3 cm), excluding clasp

TECHNIQUES

Spiral rope

Peyote stitch

26

ADDING AND ENDING THREAD

To add more thread, use a combination of weaving through the beads and tying a few half-hitch knots along the way. Don't tie any knots between the 8° spine beads because you may need to pass through these beads again and you don't want to block the holes. All knots should be tied in the loops, not the spine.

Every time you add a loop, push it to the same side before you add another loop. As a right-handed person, I push to the right. Lefties may feel more comfortable pushing to the left. Pick a side and push to that side every time!

▶ **Add the Clasp**

When figuring out the right length for your necklace or bracelet, take into account the size of the clasp you've selected. The attachment beads will add ¼ inch (6 mm) to the overall length.

1 With the thread exiting the last 8°, string three As, one half of the clasp, and three As. (Some clasp holes will allow the seed beads to move freely through the hole and others will not. That's why you add half of them on each side of the clasp.)

2 Pass back through one 8°, then weave through the beads of the second-to-last loop (this loop is behind the last loop in the illustration). This gets you back to the spine, where you pass through the top six

8°s, and then reinforce the whole pathway twice more (figure 3).

3 Attach the other half of the clasp the same way.

figure 3

FALLING FOR YOU NECKLACE

I have a large collection of lampwork beads, and I'm always looking for graceful ways to showcase them. The art beads star in this necklace, embraced by classic pearls and spiral stitch.

SUPPLIES

Size 6° Picasso blue gray Czech seed beads, 18 grams

Size 11° amber/Montana lined round seed beads, 8 grams

36 antique bronze glass pearls, 6 mm

170 antique bronze glass pearls, 3 mm

2 lampwork spacer beads, 8 mm

3 lampwork focal beads, approximately 25 mm

Toggle clasp

Size 12 beading needles

Beading thread

Beading mat

Scissors

FINISHED SIZE

21 inches (53.3 cm), excluding clasp and tassel

TECHNIQUE

Spiral rope

► Create the Tassel Section

1 Create a simple spiral rope using four 6°s for the spine and loops consisting of two 11°s, one 6-mm pearl, and two 11°s. Make seven spiral loops.

2 With the thread exiting the last 6°, string twenty 11°s and pass back through the last five 6°s. Weave through the second-to-last spiral loop and then the last 6° again to get in position to create another loop of fringe with twenty 11°s (figure 1). Make a total of four fringe loops.

3 Weave back up through the spine to exit the last 6° on the opposite end. To fill in the top of the spiral, string two 11°s, one 6-mm pearl, and two 11°s and pass through only the last three 6°s.

► Attach the Center Focal Bead

1 String one lampwork spacer bead, one 6°, the lampwork focal bead for the center dangle, one 6°, one lampwork spacer bead, and three 6°s. Make one loop off the top three 6°s with two 11°s, one 6-mm pearl, and two 11°s (figure 2).

2 After this "short stitch," work spiral rope off the top four 6° beads until you have added 13 spiral loops total (including the short loop). Add one more short stitch at the top of the section for a total of 14 loops.

3 With the thread exiting the center focal lampwork bead, create another section that is 14 loops long for the other side of the necklace, beginning and ending with short stitches.

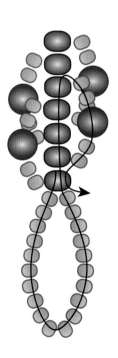

One side of this focal bead features a heart surrounded by tendrils of ivy, while the other side (shown in the photo opposite) has a dragonfly.

figure 1

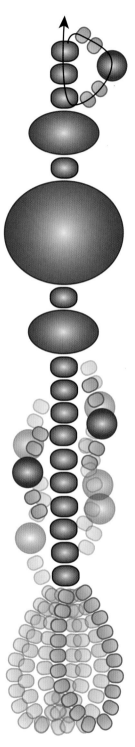

figure 2

TIP

At several points while you're working these lower sections, reinforce the thread paths all the way back down through the lampwork beads, turning around in a loop and working your way back up to where you're adding more spine beads. You want to have at least four passes of thread reinforcing these sections.

▶ Attach the Side Focal Beads

1 Pick up a lampwork bead and three 6°s. Make a short stitch over three 6°s with two 11°s, one 3-mm pearl, and two 11°s (figure 3). Continue making spiral rope using the same loop over four 6°s until you reach the desired length (sample shows 84 spiral loops).

2 Repeat on the other half of the necklace.

▶ Attach the Clasp

1 With the thread exiting the last 6° in the spine, string four 11°s, one half of the clasp, and four 11°s. Pass back down through the last five 6°s in the spine, then up through the second-to-last loop and the last 6° in the spine (figure 4). Reinforce this path at least twice more.

2 Repeat on the other end of the necklace to attach the other half of the clasp.

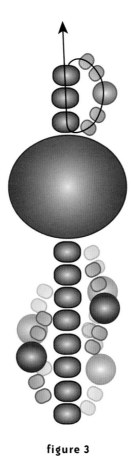

figure 3

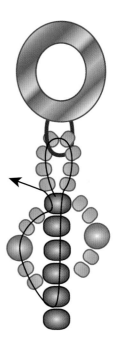

figure 4

FLIRTATION BRACELET

This piece has a cleverly hidden clasp and a flirty, asymmetrical sparkly fringe. What else does a girl need to make her happy?

► Bead the Clasp

To properly gauge the length of this brace-let, you'll make the clasp first and then work the ropes off of the finished clasp.

Top of Clasp

1 Create a piece of RAW using 11° rounds with one bead per side in each unit—the finished piece is six units wide by eight units tall.

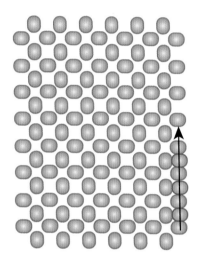

figure 1

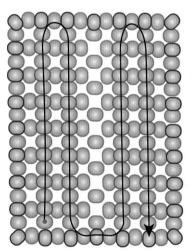

figure 2

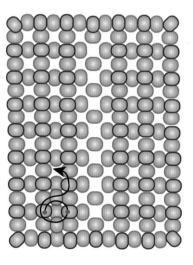

figure 3

2 With the thread exiting a bead on the outside edge, pick up one 11° round and pass through the next edge 11° (figure 1). Continue filling in spots all the way around the outside edge.

3 Weave through the beadwork so the thread exits the first inside column bead (shown with a red dot in figure 2) and stitch in the ditch along the entire column by picking up one 11° round and passing through the next 11° in the base. When you reach the end of the column, turn around and stitch in the ditch along the second column also. Bypass the middle column and weave over to stitch in the ditch along the fourth and fifth columns (figure 2).

4 With the thread exiting one of the beads added in step 3 (red dot in figure 3), pick up one 11° round and pass through the adjacent bead added in step 3 (also with red dot in figure 3). Pick up one 11° round and pass again through the first bead you exited to create a RAW unit. Continue add-ing RAW units using the existing second layer of beads all the way up the column.

SUPPLIES

Size 11° 24-karat gold electroplate round seed beads, 4 grams

43 turquoise AB2X crystal bicones, 3 mm

Size 15° 24-karat gold electroplate round seed beads, 6 grams

Size 11° gold-lined crystal cylinder beads, 3 grams

2 sew-on snaps, ¼ inch (6 mm)

Size 12 beading needles

Beading thread

Beading mat

Scissors

FINISHED SIZE

Open, 8 inches (20.3 cm), not including fringe; closed, 7½ inches (19 cm) in circumference

TECHNIQUES

Spiral rope

RAW

5 With the thread exiting the first inside edge RAW bead (one of the beads added in step 3), pick up one 11° round, one crystal, and one 11° round. Pass through the first inside edge bead of the second layer on the other side of the open center column. Pick up one 11° round, one crystal, and one 11° round. Pass through the bead first exited and the first three added in this step (figure 4). Continue adding RAW units in this way until you have filled in the center column.

6 Repeat step 4 to add RAW units to the column to the right of the middle (figure 5).

7 Securely stitch half of the two snaps to the underside along the center of the piece. Make at least four passes of thread at each intersection to reinforce.

▶ Add the Fringe

With the thread exiting an outside edge bead on the RAW units added in step 6, string ten 15°s, then (one crystal and five 15°s) four times, then one crystal and one 15°. Pass back through the

last crystal added, then string five 15°s; pass back through the next crystal and string five 15°s; continue until you reach the last crystal added, then pass back through the ten 15°s and the 11° on the clasp (figure 6). Move to the next 11° on the top layer of RAW and repeat. Continue until you have added a fringe to each RAW unit added in step 6, seven fringes total.

Bottom of Clasp

1 Create a piece of RAW using 11° rounds with one bead per side in each unit—the finished piece is seven units wide by eight units tall.

2 Repeat step 2 of the top of the clasp.

3 Stitch the other half of the two snaps along the center, making sure they align with the snaps on the other half of the clasp. The bottom half of the clasp will be one RAW unit wider than the top half.

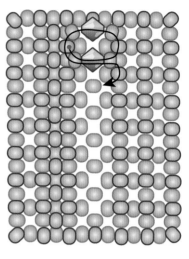

figure 4

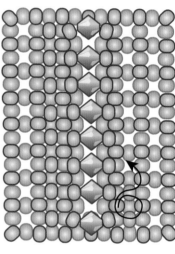

figure 5

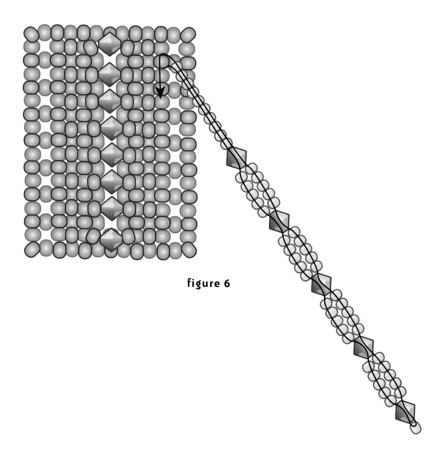

figure 6

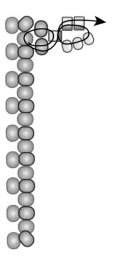

figure 7

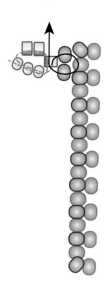

figure 8

▶ Bead the Spiral Ropes

1 With the thread exiting the edge 11° of the first RAW unit on the clasp top (along the edge opposite the fringes), string one 11° round, one 11° cylinder, and one 11° round, then pass again through the 11° on the clasp edge, creating a RAW unit. Weave through the beads so the thread exits the cylinder bead and string two more cylinder beads and three 15°s.

2 Using three cylinders for the spine and three 15°s for the loops, work spiral rope to the desired length (figure 7).

3 Pass back through all the cylinder beads to tighten up the tension. Reinforce the initial attachment point, then pass back through all the cylinder beads one more time. Add more length if necessary, since tightening up the tension can make the rope significantly shorter.

4 To attach the spiral rope to the clasp bottom, weave through the beadwork so the thread exits the last cylinder bead on the rope. Pick up one 11° round and pass through the corresponding 11° on the outside edge of the clasp bottom; pick up one 11° and pass through the cylinder bead (figure 8). Reinforce the attachment point at least twice more.

5 Attach a spiral rope to every other 11° along the edge of the top half of the clasp, for a total of four ropes.

TIP

The top and bottom halves of the clasp must be aligned properly so that the rope between them is straight. I find it easiest to attach the rope to the bottom half with the clasp snapped shut.

WINDING ROAD BRACELET

A basic spiral rope gets an upgrade with a sinuous line of pearls hiding the spine. If you want to add extra glitz, you could use 3-mm fire-polished beads or crystals in place of the pearls.

► Bead the Base Rope

Create a simple spiral rope using four 8°s for the spine and one 11°, one fire-polished, and one 11° for the loops (figure 1). Continue until you have the desired length.

► Embellish the Rope

Skipping the first 8° of the spine and exiting the second 8°, pick up one pearl and one 15°. Pass back through the pearl and through the next 8° on the spine (figure 2). Continue until you have added a pearl between every pair of 8°s except the first and last.

► Attach the Clasp

With the thread exiting the last 8° of the spine, string four 15°s, one half of the clasp, and four more 15°s. Pass back down through the last five 8°s of the spine, up through the second-to-last loop, and then through the last 8° of the spine (figure 3). String four more 15°s, pass through the clasp loop, and then string four more 15°s and repeat the previous thread path. You'll have two loops of 15°s sitting side by side for the clasp attachment. Reinforce the path at least twice more.

Repeat on the other end of the bracelet to attach the other half of the clasp.

figure 1

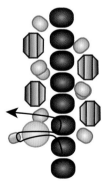

figure 2

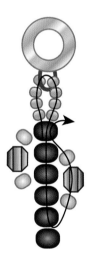

figure 3

SUPPLIES

Size 8° matte gray AB round seed beads, 3 grams

Size 11° ice blue silver-lined round seed beads, 2 grams

84 Montana blue iris Czech fire-polished rounds, 3 mm*

Size 15° gray luster iris round seed beads, 1 gram

84 peacock gray freshwater potato-shaped pearls, 3.4–4 mm*

Toggle clasp

Size 12 beading needles

Beading thread

Beading mat

Scissors

* For a bracelet 7 inches (17.8 cm) long; should you want to adjust the length, know that you'll need 12 fire-polished rounds and 12 pearls for every inch (2.5 cm) of spiral rope.

FINISHED SIZE

7 inches (17.8 cm), excluding clasp

TECHNIQUES

Spiral rope

Embellishment

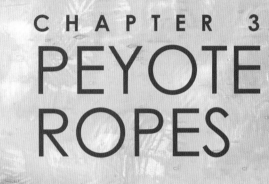

CHAPTER 3
PEYOTE
ROPES

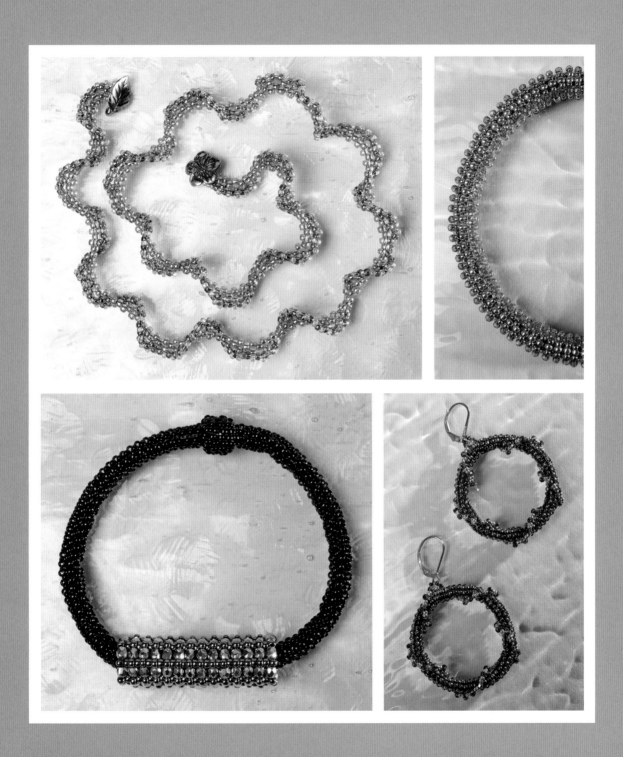

BALI DREAMING BRACELET

This gorgeous free-floating slider softly shifts over the underlying rope as you move. A magnetic clasp hidden by flared ends ensures the slider won't accidentally become separated from the base. Create a longer base rope for a matching necklace version.

▶ Bead the Peyote Rope

Beginning with eight As, create a tubular peyote stitch rope that is ¼ inch (6 mm) shorter than the desired finished length.

▶ Make the Peyote Cups

The magnetic clasp will be placed inside two cups formed with peyote stitch. To increase, pick up two As and pass through the next up A in the previous row; repeat three times, adding a total of 8 As, and step up through the first A added, splitting the pair. On the next row, pick up one A and pass through the second A of the pair on the previous row, then pick up one A and pass through the first A of the next pair in the previous row (figure 1); repeat three more times, adding a total of eight beads. Add two more rows of regular peyote stitch. Make a cup on the other end of the rope.

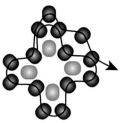

figure 1

▶ Attach the Magnetic Clasp

Weave back and forth through the As at the base of the cup and though the hole in the magnetic clasp. Make sure the clasp is tucked down into the cup and that you have passed through the clasp attachment at least four times.

SUPPLIES

Size 11° round seed beads

Color A: black, 7 grams

Color B: silver, 4 grams

98 silver Czech fire-polished beads, 3 mm

Magnetic clasp

Size 10 or 12 beading needles

Beading thread

Beading mat

Scissors

FINISHED SIZE

8½ inches (21.6 cm) long, including clasp

TECHNIQUES

Peyote stitch

RAW

► Add the Slider

1 Create a flat piece of RAW using one B, one fire-polished bead, one B, and one fire-polish bead in each unit; make the piece 14 units long by six units high (figure 2).

2 Add one last row of RAW units to join the flat piece into a circle around the peyote tube as follows. With the thread exiting a B on the long edge, fold the beadwork around the peyote tube. Pick up one fire-polished bead and pass through the B on the opposite edge of the beadwork; pick up one fire-polished bead and pass through the B you first exited (figure 3). Continue working in RAW units along the open edge to create the slider.

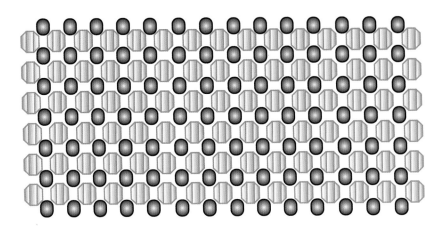

figure 2

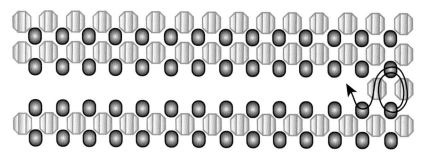

figure 3

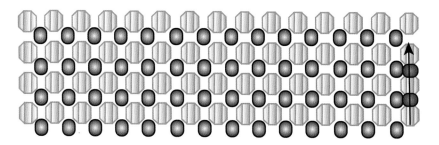

figure 4

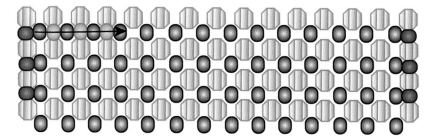

figure 5

3 Embellish the slider by adding a B in the RAW intersections and between the fire-polished beads on the outside edges as follows. With the thread exiting a fire-polished bead on one outside edge, pick up a B and pass through the next fire-polished bead (figure 4). Repeat around the entire edge, then repeat on the other end.

4 Now stitch Bs in the ditches of the RAW units as follows. Pass through the first B in one of the rows, pick up a B, and pass through the next B in the row (figure 5). This new B will sit slightly higher than the Bs in the original row. Repeat along the entire row, and then along each remaining row.

HEAVENLY HOOP EARRINGS

A classic hoop earring is something every woman should have in her jewelry wardrobe,

and here I've made it a little more fabulous with some texture and sparkle.

▶ Bead the Base Rope

Make a peyote stitch tube starting with eight As. Work for 120 rows, then join into a ring as follows.

▶ Join the Ends

Here's a little trick that will help out immensely with the challenge of joining the ends, which can make you feel like you're all thumbs.

1 Locate the bead the thread is exiting and follow that column all the way down to the opposite end of the tube; tie a small piece of thread to that bead with a simple overhand knot. You're going to remove the knot later, so don't get carried away with your knotting skills—you just need to mark this bead in some manner so you can match the ends up properly.

Note: Make sure one end of the row has an up bead and the other end of the row has a down bead (figure 1). If not, you'll need to add one more row to the working end.

2 Using the thread that's exiting the bead of the last row, pass through the bead you marked on the opposite end and again through the exited bead in a circular fashion (figure 2).

figure 1

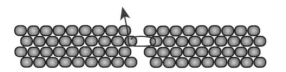

figure 2

SUPPLIES

Size 15° round seed beads

  Color A: purple metallic iris, 4 grams

  Color B: gold plated, 2 grams

80 tanzanite light vitrial crystal rounds, 2 mm

2 closed jump rings, 4 mm

2 ear wires

Size 12 beading needles

Beading thread

Beading mat

Scissors

FINISHED SIZE

Each, 1½ inches (3.8 cm) in diameter

TECHNIQUE

Peyote stitch

3 Move to the bead next to the one just exited and repeat step 2, joining it to the corresponding bead on the opposite end. Continue around, one bead at a time, until you've joined all the beads together and formed a ring.

▶ Embellish the Ring

1 Pick up two Bs and pass through the second bead on an upward diagonal (figure 3). Continue until you've beaded the entire ring.

2 With the thread exiting two Bs, pick up one crystal and pass through the next set of Bs (figure 4). Continue all the way around the ring, ending by passing through the first two Bs exited. You'll need to pull firmly to get the crystal popped into place, but be careful you don't let the crystal cut the thread.

I like to reinforce the entire embellishment, settling the crystals in place and making everything more secure.

▶ Attach the Ear Wire

With the thread exiting two Bs where you want the top of your earring to be, pick up four Bs and one jump ring; pass back through the two Bs. Reinforce this path at least twice more if possible. Attach the jump ring to an ear wire.

Repeat all steps to make a second earring.

figure 3

figure 4

RAY OF LIGHT BANGLE

Although the cross section of this bracelet is square, there's actually a round tube underneath with the embellishment providing the deceptive shaping! I've provided both bangle and clasp variations so you can make it the way you'd like.

SUPPLIES

Size 11° permanent galvanized gold round seed beads, 7.5 grams

Size 15° 24k gold-plated round seed beads, 3 grams

400 round Swarovski crystals, 2 mm

Clasp (optional)

Size 12 beading needles

Beading thread

Beading mat

Scissors

FINISHED SIZE

Interior circumference, 7½ inches (19 cm)

TECHNIQUE

Peyote stitch

HOW TO CALCULATE BANGLE LENGTH

You'll need to make the bangle large enough to slip over your hand, but not so large that it'll fall off when you wear it. To measure the tube against your hand, tuck your thumb into the center of your palm and test the tube around the thickest part of your hand, usually along the knuckles.

▶ Bead the Rope

Create a peyote stitch tube, starting with eight 11° seed beads. Continue to the desired length. You then have two choices: join the ends and embellish, as shown in the version on the facing page, or embellish and then add a clasp as shown on page 47.

▶ Join the Ends

Here's a little trick that will help out immensely with the challenge of joining the ends, which can make you feel like you're all thumbs.

1 Locate the bead the thread is exiting and follow that column all the way down to the opposite end of the tube; tie a small piece of thread to that bead with a simple overhand knot. You're going to remove the knot later, so don't get carried away with your knotting skills—you just need to mark this bead in some manner so you can match the ends up properly. Note: Make sure one end of the row has an up bead, and the other end of the row has a down bead (figure 1). If not, you'll need to add one more row to the working end.

2 Using the thread that's exiting the bead of the last row, pass through the bead you marked on the opposite end and again through the exited bead in a circular fashion (figure 2).

3 Move to the bead next to the one just exited and repeat step 2, joining it to the corresponding bead on the opposite end with the thread tied on. Continue around, one bead at a time, until you've joined all the beads together.

4 Try your bangle on. It should fit over your hand with just a bit of resistance. You'll be adding beads that will narrow the opening a little bit, so make sure it's not so tight that you won't be able to make it any smaller. But you do want it to be a little snug so it won't fall off. If you need to add more length, undo the join and bead a few more rows.

If your joined spot is loosey-goosey (and it very well may be), reinforce it by stitching around again.

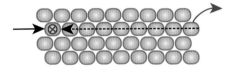

figure 1

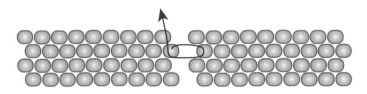

figure 2

► Embellish the Bangle

You can start the embellishment anywhere on the bangle.

1 With the thread exiting an 11° bead, string one 15°, one crystal, and one 15°; stitch in the ditch by passing through the next 11° with the hole oriented in the same direction, laying your new beads across the ditch between the 11°s (figure 3).

2 Pass through the 11° next to the bead you are exiting in the reverse direction. String one 15°, one crystal, and one 15°, and then stitch in the ditch by passing through the next 11° with the hole oriented in the same direction (figure 4). Repeat this step along the entire length of the rope.

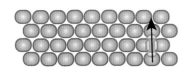

figure 3

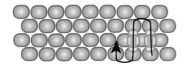

figure 4

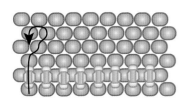

figure 5

VARIATION: You can make this design with or without a clasp.

3 To weave to the next row, pass through two 11°s on an upward diagonal, then pass through the first 11° horizontally in the opposite direction (figure 5).

4 Repeat steps 1 through 3 to embellish along the entire length of the rope four times total.

► Add a Clasp

If you're making the clasped version, make the peyote tube the final desired bracelet length minus the width of the clasp. Begin the embellishment on the second row from the edge. You can either work back across the rope in the opposite direction from the previous row or you can flip the rope over to continue working in the same direction.

► Attach the Clasp

1 With the thread exiting an outside edge up bead, peyote stitch around using two 15°s in each stitch. Step up through the first two 15°s. Peyote stitch around with one 15° in each stitch. Without adding any more beads, reinforce the last four 15°s, pulling them to the center.

2 String a small loop of 15°s to go through the clasp attachment and pass back through the 15° opposite the bead exited in the last set of four. Reinforce this path at least two more times. Repeat on the other end with the other half of the clasp.

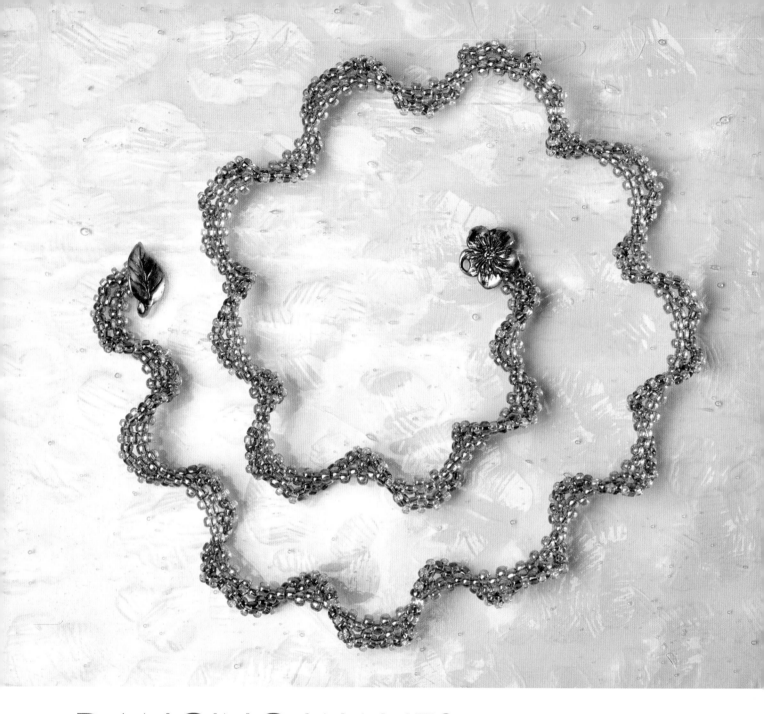

DANCING WAVES NECKLACE

Simple is elegant. The rolling curl of this necklace is straightforward and quick to make, yet it produces a stylish statement—not overpowering but not invisible, either. Mission accomplished.

▶ Bead the Peyote Rope

1 Cut a piece of thread about 2 yards (1.8 m) long and wind half the thread onto a bobbin. You'll use this second length when the working thread needs to be ended.

2 String enough As to measure the desired necklace length, and then add another inch (2.5 cm) of beads to compensate for shrinkage as the piece spirals.

3 Peyote stitch the entire length with As, then peyote stitch the entire length with two Bs in each stitch (figure 1). The rope will start to bend and spiral—this is okay! It's what we want to happen, so encourage it instead of trying to straighten it out.

4 Peyote stitch the entire length with one 11° in each stitch and one 11° between each of the two beads added in step 3 (figure 2).

Turn and coil the rope to encourage the spiraling action and make the waves flow in the same direction.

▶ Attach the Clasp

With the thread exiting an A bead at one end, string a small loop of 11°s to go through the clasp attachment and pass back through the A bead you exited. Reinforce this path at least twice more. Repeat on the other end with the other half of the clasp.

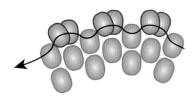

figure 1

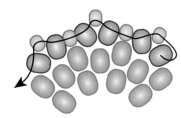

figure 2

SUPPLIES

Size 8° round seed beads

 Color A: ice blue gold luster, 12 grams

 Color B: gray AB, 7 grams

Size 11° shimmering soft sage–lined round seed beads, 5 grams

Clasp

Size 12 beading needles

Beading thread

Beading mat

Scissors

FINISHED SIZE

18½ inches (47 cm), excluding clasp

TECHNIQUE

Peyote stitch

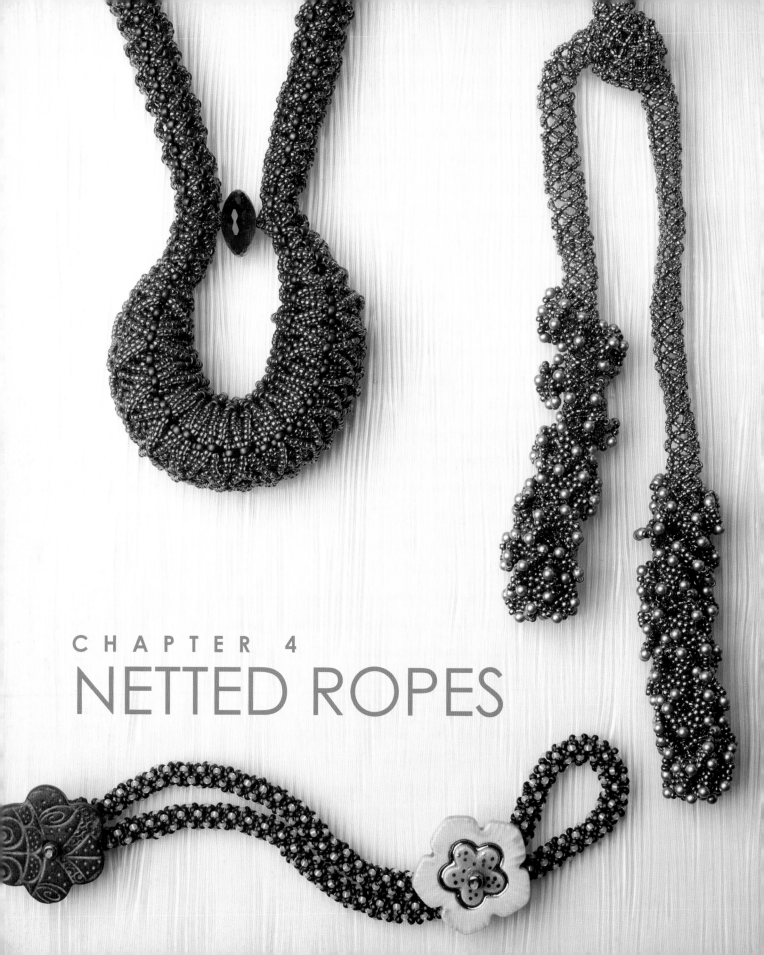

CHAPTER 4
NETTED ROPES

JOSEPHINE'S FORTUNE NECKLACE

You'll start out by creating two very long netted ropes and then you'll tie them together in a Josephine's knot. Add peyote stitch end caps, rope detail, and a clasp, then finish it off with a tassel. It's a bunch of pieces, but together they're stunning!

► Bead the Ropes for the Knot

Make two ropes with size 11° beads, one bronze and one blue, using the netting technique with a step up; each rope should be about 34 inches (86.4 cm) long. Start with 12 beads in a ring; *string three beads, skip three beads, and pass through the next bead on the ring; repeat from * once more; step up through the first two beads added. Continue making three wings of three beads each for each row. Don't tie off your thread when you reach the desired length—you'll be adding more rows after the knot is tied.

► Tie the Knot

You'll tie the knot now even though the ropes are not yet full length. The reason for this is that each beader will tie the knot with a different tension, and the tightness will affect the rope length. Additionally, after tying the knot, the ropes will have different lengths remaining because the rope on the outside edge of the knot will use up more length than the rope on the inside edge. You'll even them out after you complete the knot. You may have to tie your knot several times to get it right—I still do! Have patience.

1 Place the ropes side by side on a flat surface. You'll treat them as one. It can be tricky, so take your time. About two-thirds of the way down the ropes, pick up what will be the left side and loop it up and over the right side (figure 1). The left side of the rope is the longer one.

2 With the long end, create another loop that sits on top of the first loop, then tuck the end of this rope under the short rope (figure 2).

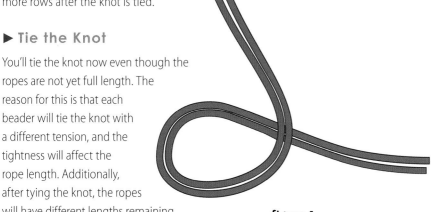

figure 1

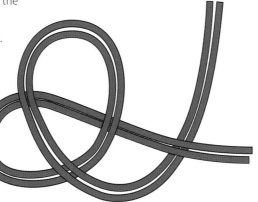

figure 2

SUPPLIES

Size 11° round seed beads

    Color A: bronze metallic, 80 grams

    Color B: amethyst/dark blue lined, 60 grams

Size 15° midnight blue metallic round seed beads, 2 grams

2 bronze round or freshwater potato-shaped pearls, 4 mm

Size 10 or 12 beading needles

Beading thread

Beading mat

Scissors

FINISHED SIZE

Knot, 3 inches (7.6 cm) wide and 2¼ inches (5.7 cm) tall, excluding tassel

Attachment ropes, each 9 inches (22.9 cm) long, excluding clasp

TECHNIQUES

Netting with step up

Peyote stitch

3 Last step! With the long rope, which is coming from under the short rope, weave over the right side of the top loop, under the right side of the bottom loop, over the left side of the top loop, and under the left side of the bottom loop (figure 3).

Gently tug here and there to tighten up the knot. Make sure the ropes don't move on top of each other and bunch up—they should sit nicely side by side along the whole knot.

► Tack the Knot

When you've got your knot looking like you want it, start a new thread in one of the ropes; this thread should exit a bead near one of the major knot intersections (where one rope crosses another).

There's no magic to this—you're simply sewing the ropes together. Pass the needle through the rope your thread is attached to, then through the rope under

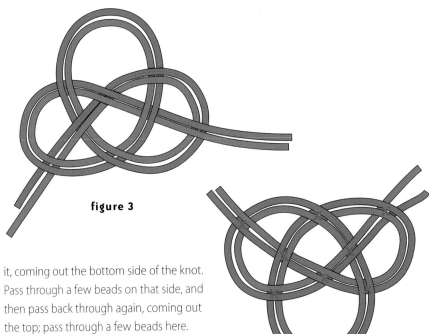

figure 3

figure 4

it, coming out the bottom side of the knot. Pass through a few beads on that side, and then pass back through again, coming out the top; pass through a few beads here. Keep sewing the intersection together until you feel that it's secure—I usually do about four passes. Now weave through the beadwork until you get to another major intersection and do the same thing. There are about eight major intersections, but I rarely reinforce all of them. Five or six will work just fine (figure 4).

► Finish the Attachment Ropes

Work netting stitch to even out the rope ends and make them the length you need. Keep in mind that the clasp will add about 2 inches (5.1 cm) to the length of your piece.

► Make the End Caps and Tubes

1 Using a new length of thread (an arm's length will do), string 24 As. Leaving a 4- to 6-inch (10.2 to 15.2 cm) tail, pass through the first eight or nine beads again to form a ring. Peyote stitch around the ring with A, stepping up at the end of each row; repeat for a total of nine rows.

2 Now you'll decrease to make a flat top on the end cap. On row 10, skip a spot where you'd normally add a bead and just pass through the next up bead instead (figure 5). Tighten firmly toward the inside of the circle. Don't worry if a lot of thread shows because as you continue, it will disappear into the beads.

Make two more regular peyote stitches, then skip a spot again. You're making the corners right now, so the decreases need to be evenly spaced. Make two more peyote stitches, skip one space, make two more peyote stitches, skip one space, and make two more peyote stitches. (You've decreased four beads.) For your step up on this round, move across that intersection where there's only thread, and step up through the next two beads (figure 6).

ADDING AND ENDING THREAD

Add new thread at the end of a row so that the new thread can exit the middle bead of a netted wing. Pass on a diagonal through a couple of beads, and then tie a surgeon's knot. This is the same as a half-hitch knot, but you go through the loop twice instead of once. Then pass through a few more beads and make another knot. If you're adding a thread, pass through the center bead of a wing. If you're ending a thread, pass through a few more beads and cut the thread.

3 Work one row even, making normal peyote stitches all the way around, including adding a bead in the V-shaped gap, adding eight beads total. Step up and pull tightly. Yep, the top will start to fold over now!

4 Add four beads in the last row: Pick up a bead, pass over the V-shaped gap, and pass through the second up bead. Repeat to add three more beads. I like to reinforce this row by going around with my thread one more time.

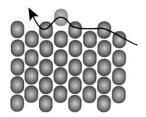

figure 5

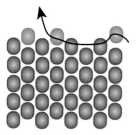

figure 6

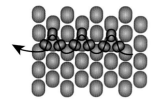

figure 7

5 To embellish the end cap, pass through the beadwork to exit a bead on the side of the straight section, roughly halfway down. Officially, it's Row 5, but just eyeball it and pick a place you think looks good. String three 15°s and pass through the next A on that same row (stitch in the ditch). Add a set of three 15°s between each bead in that row (figure 7). The 15°s will create a pretty picot around the end cap.

If you have thread left over when you're finished, weave it down to the bottom of the end cap. You can use it later to attach the end cap to the ropes. If the working thread is short, end it off and attach a new one later.

6 Make a total of three end caps (one for each side of the clasp, and one for the top of the tassel) and then make two tubes for side embellishment on your ropes. The tubes are worked the same as the end caps through Row 9.

▶ Make the Clasp

This consists of a beaded toggle bar that latches into a beaded ring.

Bead the Toggle Bar

1 Create a peyote toggle bar with As by making a peyote stitch strip beginning with 20 beads for rows 1 and 2, and beading a total of 10 rows. Zip the last row to the first to create a tube, then drop your needle down through the center of the toggle bar. Exiting the tube opening,

VARIATION

So much in a hurry to wear this necklace that you don't want to take the time to make the tassel? That's okay. Here's how it would look.

string one pearl and three 15°s; pass back through the pearl (the 15°s will create a picot on the end) and through the tube, coming out the opposite end (figure 8).

2 Add a pearl and picot embellishment to this end of the tube. If possible, pass back through the pearl and picot beads on each end one more time to reinforce them. You may not be able to get through the pearl again, but try. End your thread.

figure 8

▶ Bead the Toggle Ring

1 Using a new 3-foot (91.4 m) length of thread, string fifty 15°s. Leaving a 4- to 6-inch (10.2 to 15.2 cm) tail, pass through the first 10 beads to form a ring. Peyote stitch around the ring with 15°s, stepping up at the end of each row, until you have a total of five rows.

2 Using As, add another four rows. Pass through the beadwork to exit a 15° on the opposite side of the ring, and add another three rows of As. Finally, zip up the end rows of As together.

3 Add picot embellishments as for the end caps: Exiting an A bead on the outside edge, string three 15°s and pass through the next A in that same row. Add a set of three 15°s between every bead in the row.

▶ Attach the End Caps and Clasp

1 Slide the decorative tubes over the two ropes. These can either float freely or you can stitch them into place.

2 Insert two rope ends into an end cap, side by side. With the thread exiting a bead on the bottom edge of the end cap, pass down into the rope directly beneath the exit bead and pass through a few beads in the rope. Pass through a couple of end cap beads, then through a couple of rope beads. Zigzag around the end caps and ropes until everything is secure. Pass through the beadwork so the thread exits the top of the end cap.

3 To attach the bar side of the toggle, string 12 As, pass through two middle beads of the toggle bar, and then string another 12 As. Pass through the opposite seed bead from where you exited the end cap. Reinforce this path at least two more times, and then end off your thread.

4 To attach the loop side of the toggle, string 20 As and the toggle ring. Pass through the opposite seed bead from where you exited the end cap hole—the 20 As will form a loop to hold the ring. Pass back through the first bead and make a second loop of 20 As. The second loop helps distribute the weight pulling on the end cap as you wear the necklace. Reinforce both loops at least one more time.

▶ Make the Tassel

1 Using about 24 inches (61 cm) of thread, string eight As; pass through the beads again to form a ring, then tie a knot to secure it. Leave the thread attached so you can use it to join the tassel to the necklace later.

2 Using a new length of about 18 inches (45.7 cm) of thread, center and tie the thread on the ring of As with a square knot, creating two lengths of 9 inches (22.9 cm) each. This doesn't have to be pretty and it's okay if the knot ends up on top of the As—it will all be covered with an end cap. The circle of As is just a structural piece to hold the tassel strands.

3 Thread a needle onto one strand and string enough As to create the tassel length you like. I used 40, but you can certainly use more or fewer to get the look you want. Then string three 15°s and pass back up through about 15 to 20 As. Tie a surgeon's knot. Pass through another few beads, tie another knot, and then pass through a few last beads and end off the thread.

4 Continue adding strands until you achieve the fullness you want. As the tassel starts getting full, check to see how it looks with your end cap on top. I made a total of 16 strands for the sample.

▶ Connect the Tassel

To connect the tassel to the necklace, use the thread you left on the tassel ring, and pass through the center hole in the last end cap. String seven As and then pass through the Josephine's knot ropes where you'd like to place the tassel. Pass through the beadwork to the middle of the knot and pass through several seed beads in one of the ropes, then work back to the tassel; pass back through the seven As, around the top of the end cap, and back up into the knot. Make at least three passes between the knot and the tassel to reinforce this connection, and then end off your thread.

Note: Don't attach the tassel just to the bottom two tubes on the Josephine's knot—this will leave all the weight of the tassel supported by those two tubes alone, and they could stretch out. By working up into the center of the knot, you're distributing the weight and making it more secure.

ABUNDANCE
NECKLACE

Layers of netting create a visual feast and compel you to focus on the details. The inner core gives the necklace depth and also functions as an armature for the layers of netted weave. The dramatic U shape brings to mind a vessel full of beady goodness.

SUPPLIES

Size 11° lavender rose gold luster round seed beads, 80 grams

Size 8° black purple matte metallic iris round seed beads, 40 grams

Amethyst rondelle, approximately 17 x 10 mm

Size 10 or 12 beading needles

Beading thread

Beading mat

Scissors

FINISHED SIZE

36 inches (91.4 cm) long and 3 inches (7.6 cm) around at widest point

TECHNIQUES

Netting with step up

Peyote stitch

▶ **Bead the Inner Rope**

1 To create a netted rope, string two 11°s and one 8°; repeat five more times for a total of 18 beads; pass through the beads again to form a ring. With the thread exiting an 8°, pick up a wing of two 11°s, one 8°, and two 11°s; skip one 8° and pass through the next 8° on the ring; repeat two more times and step up through the first two 11°s and one 8° added. Continue netting with a step up at the end of each row until you have made a rope that's the desired finished length.

2 To join the ends, pick up two 11°s and pass through the corresponding 8° on the opposite end of the rope. Pick up two 11°s and pass through the next 8° wing bead on the original end of the rope (figure 1). Continue zigzagging back and forth between the 8°s with two 11°s until you have completed the join.

▶ **Bead the Outer Rope**

With the thread exiting an 8° bead on the inner rope, string three 11°s and one 8°; repeat four more times, then pick up two more 11°s. Pass through the 8° originally exited, and step up through the first three 11°s and one 8°. Make wings of three 11°s, one 8°, and three 11°s to create the outer rope, which is stitched in on the first row and then floats on top of the inner rope. Join the ends as you did with the inner rope.

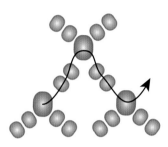

figure 1

▶ Embellish

You'll build layers of netting on top of the inner and outer ropes, with each layer's wings holding progressively more 11°s. Attach the first and last row of each subsequent layer to the previous layer, but allow the remainder of the layer being worked to float above the rope.

1 With the thread exiting an 8° on the outer rope, string four 11°s, one 8°, and four 11°s. Pass through the next 8° on the outer rope; repeat two more times and step up. Work netting with wings of four 11°s, one 8°, and four 11°s for approximately 5½ inches (14 cm). On the last row of this layer, string four 11°s, pass through an 8° on the outer rope, and string four more 11°s for the wing—so instead of picking up an 8° in the middle of the wing as usual, you'll pass through an 8° in the previous layer.

2 With the thread exiting an 8° of the last layer added—not the 8° on the outer rope, but from one set of 8°s inward—string five 11°s, one 8°, and five 11°s and pass through the next 8° of the previous layer; repeat two more times and step up. Work netting with wings of five 11°s, one 8°, and five 11°s until you are one row shy of where you ended the previous layer; on the last row of this layer, string five 11°s and pass through an 8° on the previous layer; repeat all the way around the row.

Continue building layers in this manner, each time moving one set of beads inward on each end to create a graduated effect, and each time using one more 11° in each set until you have wings with seven 11°s.

▶ Attach the Rondelle

With the thread exiting an 8° approximately three rows away from the embellishment, pick up the rondelle; while bending the embellished section of the rope, pass through the corresponding 8° three rows away from the embellishment on the opposite side. Reinforce this path as many times as you can—it will get a lot of wear and tear and you don't want it to break.

FLOWER POWER BRACELET

Show off pretty flower buttons with a unique double-loop closure.

No need to hide the clasp here—it's the focal point!

► Bead the Base Rope

1 String one A and one B six times for a total of 12 beads; pass through all beads again to form a ring. With the thread exiting a B, string one A, one B, and one A; skip one B on the ring and pass through the second B (figure 1). Repeat twice to make three wings; step up through the first A and B of the first wing added (figure 2).

2 Continue adding rows with three wings consisting of A, B, A, passing through the B of the previous row's wing, and stepping up at the end of the row by passing through the first A and B added until the bracelet is the desired length (see below).

► Join the Rope Ends

When your rope is the desired length, join the two ends to form a circle by picking up one A and passing through the B on the other half of the rope, and then repeating all the way around (figure 3).

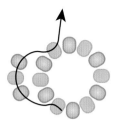

figure 1

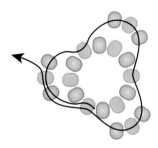

figure 2

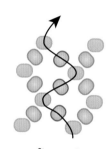

figure 3

SUPPLIES

Size 11° round seed beads

> Color A: copper matte metallic iris, 15 grams

> Color B: candlelight opal, 7.5 grams

2 size 6° bronze metallic round seed beads

2 porcelain flower buttons, approximately 1¼ inches (3.2 cm) in diameter

Size 12 beading needles

Beading thread

Beading mat

Scissors

FINISHED SIZE

Closed, 6½ inches (16.5 cm)

TECHNIQUES

Netting with step up

Peyote stitch

DETERMINING BRACELET LENGTH

This bracelet fits about 1 inch (2.5 cm) smaller than your usual length. So if you'd normally make a bracelet 7½ inches (19 cm) long, you'll want to make this one 8½ inches (21.6 cm) long.

The clasp will take up about 2½ inches (6.4 cm), requiring two 5-inch (12.7 cm) loops of rope. The area between the two connectors will comprise the rest of the length.

If you're making an 8½-inch (21.6 cm) bracelet, 2½ inches (6.4 cm) will be the clasp, which means you'll need 6 inches (15.2 cm) between the connectors. There will be two strands of rope going across that section, so you'll need 12 inches (30.5 cm) for the between-the-connectors area and 10 inches (25.4 cm) for the clasp area; your rope should measure 22 inches (55.9 cm) to make a bracelet 8½ inches (21.6 cm) long.

▶ Make the Connectors

1 Using As, create a piece with flat peyote stitch that starts with 12 beads and is 36 rows long. Zip the two ends around one folded end of the netted rope (figure 4). Position the peyote connector about 1¾ inches (4.4 cm) back from the loop end.

2 Weave through the beadwork so that the thread exits two beads in the center of the connector. Pick up two As and pass through these two beads again (figure 5). Reinforce once more to secure.

3 With the thread exiting the two As added in the previous step, pick up one flower button, one 6°, and one B, and then pass back down through the 6° and the flower button; secure by passing through the two As exited at the beginning of this step (figure 6). Repeat the path at least twice more to reinforce.

4 Repeat steps 1 through 3 on the other end of the rope.

▶ Finish

When you're sure the connector is positioned properly so the loop can go over the flower button, tack it in place. Repeat at the other end of the bracelet.

To close the clasp, feed one loop inside the other, and secure it around the flower. Secure the other loop around the opposite flower.

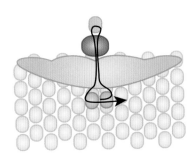

figure 5

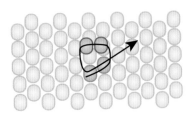

figure 6

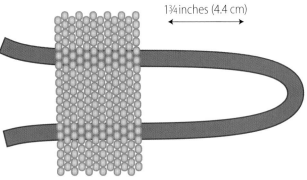

1¾ inches (4.4 cm)

figure 4

FRENCH QUARTER LARIAT

Netting without a step up creates a delicate spiral lariat, and ruffle embellishments made with netting and peyote stitch dress up the ends. My friend Marilou Porth and I talked over the idea for this piece, which I had planned for the book. She then ran with it, doing the actual designing. I love collaborations!

SUPPLIES

Size 15° steel blue gold luster iris round seed beads, 25 grams

Size 11° light bronze metallic round seed beads, 20 grams

300 bronze glass or freshwater pearls, 3 mm

Size 10 or 12 beading needles

Beading thread

Beading mat

Scissors

FINISHED SIZE

42 inches (1.1 m) long

TECHNIQUES

Netting with no step up

Peyote stitch

▶ Bead the Rope

Create a rope of netting with no step up as follows. String two 15°s and one 11° seven times; pass through the first three beads again to form a ring—the thread exits a size 11° seed bead. For the wings, string two 15°s, one 11°, and two 15°s; skip one 11° and pass through the next 11°. Continue until you have the desired length.

▶ Add the Ruffled Embellishment

1 With the thread exiting an 11° bead on the bottom of one end of the rope, string five 15°s and pass through the next 11° (figure 1). Continue stringing five 15°s and passing through the next 11° until you've gone all the way around the bottom of the rope (figure 2).

2 Now you'll work your way up the rope, adding the embellishment on a diagonal. String five 15°s and pass through the first 11° on the diagonal from the bead you exited (figure 3). Continue working on the diagonal until you've added approximately 150 stitches, or 3 to 3½ inches (7.6 to 8.9 cm).

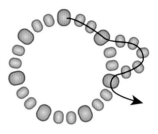

figure 1

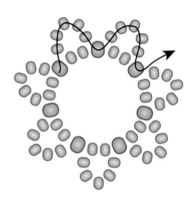

figure 2

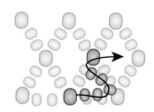

figure 3

DESIGN OPTIONS

Use 2- or 3-mm crystals or drop beads instead of pearls in the final embellishment row.

3 Tie a half-hitch knot and turn to work in the opposite direction. Pass back through the 11° last exited; peyote stitch three 11°s along the 15°s added in the last step, beginning and ending by passing through an 11° on the rope. Continue to peyote stitch each set of 15°s with 11°s along the whole line of embellishment (figure 4). For the last pass, tie a half-hitch knot and turn the work again.

4 Peyote stitch one 11°, one pearl, and one 11° between every 11° added in the previous row (figure 5). Note: The 11°s and pearl added in this row are outlined in red in figure 5.

5 Repeat the embellishment on the other end of the lariat.

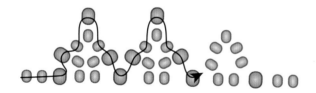

figure 4

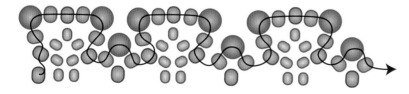

figure 5

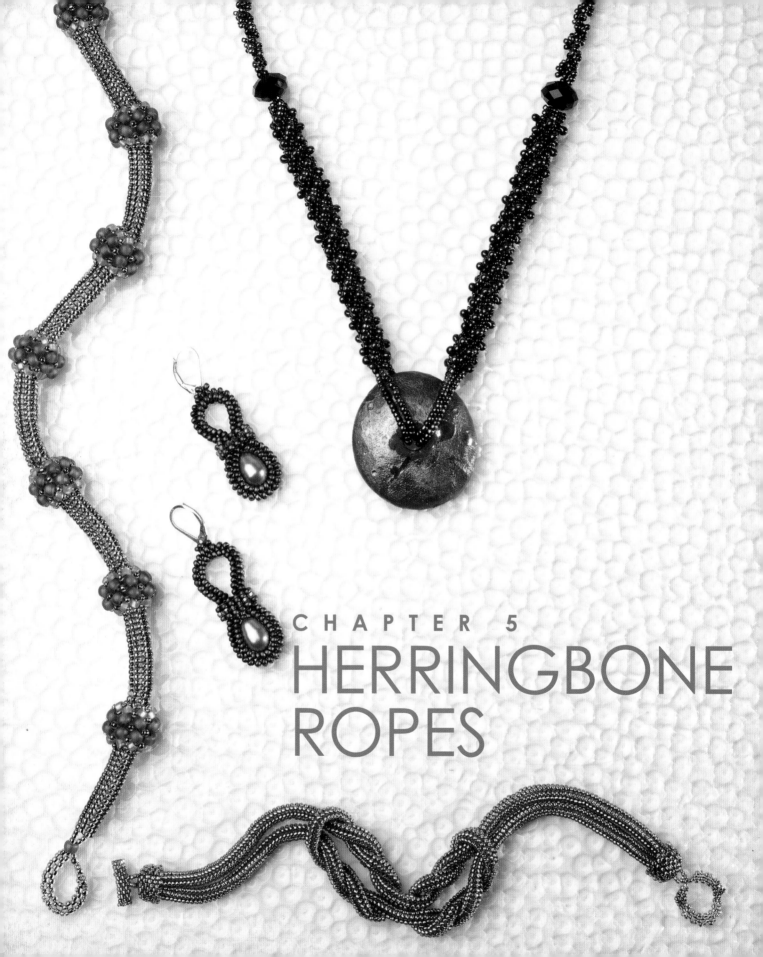

CHAPTER 5
HERRINGBONE ROPES

FOREVER TANGO
BRACELET

The way these ropes intertwine reminds me of a sensuous tango.

Intricate curves and coils make it hard to see where

one piece starts and the other ends.

▶ Make the Rings

Create two lengths of herringbone rope, three stitches (six beads) around and 60 rows long. Join the ends of each rope together to form rings. End your threads and set the two rings aside.

▶ Make the Base Ropes

Create two lengths of herringbone rope, three stitches (six beads) around. The length should be ¾ inch (1.9 cm) less than your finished bracelet length. End your threads.

▶ Weave the Rings and Base Ropes Together

Lay one ring flat on the table and pass one of the base ropes around it twice. Pass the second base rope around the other side of the ring twice—the ropes go over, under, and then over the ring (figure 1). Slide the ring onto the base ropes so that it's positioned where you want it and the rope ends are aligned evenly. Attach the second ring the same way, making sure you pass the ropes through the ring in the same pattern as for the first ring.

▶ Make the End Caps

1 Create a peyote tube starting with 24 beads for the first two rows, and bead seven rows total.

Row 8 Decrease as follows. *Make two peyote stitches, then add no bead in the next spot; repeat this decrease from * three more times; you've now finished the row. Step up to begin the next row.

Row 9 Peyote stitch around as usual (8 stitches).

Row 10 Make one peyote stitch, then skip a spot; repeat this decrease to the end of the row; step up.

Row 11 Peyote stitch around as usual (4 stitches).

2 Repeat to make a second end cap.

SUPPLIES

Size 15° round seed beads, 12 grams

Size 10 or 12 beading needles

Beading thread

Beading mat

Scissors

FINISHED SIZE

8¼ inches (21 cm) long, excluding clasp

TECHNIQUES

Ladder stitch

Herringbone stitch

Peyote stitch

69

figure 1

▶ Make the Toggle Bar

Create a toggle bar by making a peyote-stitch strip beginning with 12 beads for rows 1 and 2, and beading a total of 10 rows. Zip the last row to the first to create a tube.

▶ Attach the End Caps

1 Insert two rope ends into an end cap, side by side. With the thread exiting a bead on the bottom edge of the end cap, pass down into the rope directly beneath the exit bead and pass through a few beads in the rope. Pass through a couple of end cap beads, then through a couple of rope beads. Zigzag around the end cap and ropes until everything is secure. Pass through the beadwork so the thread exits the top of the end cap.

2 Repeat on the other side to attach the second end cap.

▶ Attach the Clasp

1 With the thread exiting one of the center beads in the top of an end cap, pick up three beads and pass through two middle beads of the toggle bar; pick up another three beads and pass through the opposite seed bead from where you exited the end cap. Reinforce this path at least two more times, and then end off the thread.

2 With the thread exiting one of the center beads in the top of the other end cap, pick up enough beads to circle the toggle bar. I used 34, but you may need to use slightly more or fewer depending on the size of your beads. Pass through the fourth bead you picked up and through the three beads below it, then back into the end cap. Weave over two beads in the end cap, and pick up three beads; pass through the fourth bead, which is now sitting sideways between the two attachments, and through the first two beads of the loop (figure 2). Peyote stitch around the loop, ending two beads shy of the forth bead. Reinforce the attachment points, weaving your way to the loop beads again. On the last pass around the loop, peyote stitch with two beads in each stitch. End your thread in the end cap.

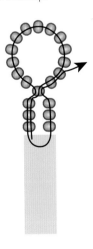

figure 2

ELEMENTAL
NECKLACE

I love putting segments of different styles of rope

together to create visually interesting combinations

and to set off special focal pieces. I think all the

elements come together just perfectly in this necklace!

SUPPLIES

**Size 15° black round
seed beads, 4 grams**

**Size 11° metallic mix round
seed beads, 14 grams**

**2.8-mm metallic dark raspberry
iris drop beads, 6.5 grams**

**Raku donut, 1½ inches (3.8 cm)
in diameter**

2 black crystal rondelles, 12 mm

Size 12 beading needles

Beading thread

Beading mat

Scissors

FINISHED SIZE

**24 inches (61 cm) long,
including clasp**

TECHNIQUES

Spiral herringbone stitch

Spiral rope

Peyote stitch

72

▶ Bead the Spiral Herringbone Rope

Rows 1 and 2 Use ladder stitch and alternate picking up two 15°s and two 11°s to create a piece that is eight columns wide; pass through the end beads with a circular thread path to join them and form a tube.

Row 3 With the thread exiting a 15°, stitch one row of regular herringbone stitch using one 15° and one 11° for each stitch and passing down through one 11° in the second row and up through one 15°. Step up at the end of the row through the first 15° added.

Row 4 Continue to use one 15° and one 11° for each stitch, but on this row you'll start to use spiral herringbone. Pick up beads and go down through two 11°s and up through one 15°. There are no more step-ups until the end of the rope.

Row 5 Pick up one 15° and one drop bead for each stitch.

Rows 6 and 7 Pick up one 15° and one 11° for each stitch.

Repeat Rows 5 through 7 until you have the length desired; my version uses 3¼-inch (8.3 cm) lengths.

To end the rope, work one row with 15°s and drops and one row with 15°s and 11°s. Then do two rows of regular herringbone stitch with 15°s and 11°s —you'll be forcing the beads to straighten up again and you'll need to step up at the end of the rows. Pass through the last two rows with a ladder stitch thread path to further straighten the beads and match the other end.

Create a second length of rope to match the first.

► Attach the Donut

1 With the thread exiting an 11° on one end of the rope, string enough 11°s to circle the donut; pass back through the first two 15°s in the third column over (leaving two empty columns). Stitch over to the next 11° column and repeat, stringing enough 11°s to circle the donut for a second line of attachment; pass back through the first two 15°s in the third column over, next to the one used for the first attachment.

2 Repeat with the second rope.

► Bead the Spiral Rope Transition

1 With the thread exiting an 11° column, string one crystal rondelle and six 11°s. Pass back down through the rondelle and into the 11° column opposite where you exited. Reinforce this path at least twice more if possible (figure 1).

2 With the thread exiting one set of three 11°s at the top of the rondelle, string four 11°s and pass through the top two 11°s of the original three exited and the first 11° added in this step (figure 2). Continue working spiral rope, using three 11°s for the core and three 11°s for the loops, until the rope is the desired length; the sample rope is 6¾ inches (17.1 cm) long.

3 Repeat on the other side of the rope.

► Bead the Clasp

1 Create a toggle bar with 11°s by making a peyote-stitch strip beginning with 10 beads for rows 1 and 2, and beading a total of 10 rows. Zip the last row to the first to create a tube.

2 With the thread exiting the last spine 11°, pick up two 11°s, pass through two center beads on a diagonal in the toggle bar, and pick up two 11°s; pass back through one 11° in the spine, and then weave through the beads of the second-to-last loop. This gets you back to the spine, where you can pass through the top four 11° beads, and then reinforce this whole pathway twice more (figure 3).

3 On the other end of the rope, string enough 11°s to circle the toggle bar (I used 25 beads—you may need to use more or fewer depending on your beads) and then pass back through the first two beads added and the first 11° in the spine (figure 4). Weave through the beads of the second-to-last loop and back up the spine beads. Reinforce this pathway twice more.

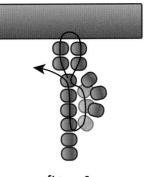

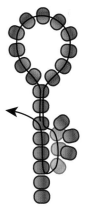

figure 3

figure 1

figure 2

figure 4

ZIGGURAT RING

A single herringbone rope, when spiraled back on itself, becomes
the perfect nest for a crystal stone. Although I've chosen to finish it
as a ring, it would also make a wonderful pendant.

SUPPLIES

Size 15° nickel silver electroplate
round seed beads, 5 grams

Jet crystal donut, 12 mm

Size 12 beading needles

Beading thread

Beading mat

Scissors

FINISHED SIZE

Pendant, approximately 1¼ inches
(3.2 cm); ring attachment as desired

TECHNIQUES

Ladder stitch

Herringbone stitch

RAW

► Make the Rope

Ladder stitch size 15° seed beads to create a strip that's two beads high by six beads long. Join the ends to form a ring; work off this ring to create a herringbone tube that's 10 inches (25.4 cm) long. You need the rope to be very flexible, so use soft tension.

► Make the Spiral Coils

Start a new thread that exits the beadwork about 1¼ inches (3.2 cm) from one end of the rope. Leaving a ¼-inch (6 mm) end free, begin coiling the rope, making the first coil about 1 inch (2.5 cm) in diameter and the next one to fit the inside circumference of the first. Work your way slowly around the coil, tacking the two sections of rope together by ladder stitching sets of two or three beads together every 10 beads or so (figure 1). As you work your way around, the coils are progressively smaller, fitting just inside each other.

► Join the Ends

After you've tacked three coils together, tuck the remaining length of rope down the center of the coils. Join the two ends of the herringbone rope together with ladder stitch.

► Add the Center Stone

Weave through the beadwork so the thread exits the center of the top coil. Attach the donut by weaving back and forth through the stone from one side of the coil to the other, passing through a few beads in the rope each time (figure 2). To make sure it's securely reinforced, I like to weave at least four passes of thread through the center stone.

figure 1

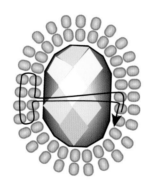

figure 2

► Make the Ring Band

Attach a new thread to the bottom coil. Make sure you have your center stone oriented the way you like—horizontally or vertically—so the ring band starts in the proper location. Create a band of RAW, using two beads per side, until it's the length you need for your ring size. To attach the band to the opposite side of the bottom coil, pick up two beads, pass through two beads in the coil, and then pick up two more beads; complete the attachment by passing through the last two beads in the final RAW unit.

► Stabilize the Ring Band

I like to add a stabilizing bead between each RAW box on the outside edges of the band. Weave through the last RAW attachment to the two beads on the coil. Pick up one seed bead and pass through the next two beads along the edge of the band (figure 3). Repeat to add a single seed bead between each two-bead section along this side of the band. Pass through the beads in the coil, and then add the single seed bead between the sections along the second edge. End the thread.

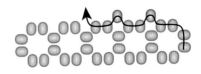

figure 3

BUBBLES AND BUMPS NECKLACE

Changing the size of the beads as you work herringbone stitch forms eye-catching bumps. The bubbled section has a hidden round bead, keeping the work expanded instead of collapsing flat. Simple trick, big payoff!

► Start the Rope

Create a tubular herringbone rope starting with eight size 11° beads (four stitches). Work 17 rows.

► Make Bumps

1 The finished necklace will have a total of 11 bumps. To create each bump seamlessly on the rope, you'll make the same herringbone stitch but with different size beads. To help cover the thread and further embellish the bump, you'll also add either an 11° or a 15° at the top and/or bottom of each stitch. Inserting an 8-mm round bead inside a bump keeps it rounded.

2 To add an embellishment bead at the top of the stitch, you'll pick up one stitch bead, one embellishment bead, and one stitch bead. Make the stitch as usual, but ignore the embellishment bead on future rows. This bead is shown at the top of figure 1.

3 To add an embellishment bead on the bottom of the stitch, after you've added the stitch beads and passed down through the bead on the previous row, you'll pick up one embellishment bead and then pass up through the bead in the next set of beads to finish the stitch. This bead is the second one added in figure 1.

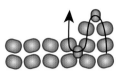

figure 1

Note: The beadwork will all be loosey-goosey and flare outward as you change bead sizes—this is normal! The bump tightens up at the end of the sequence.

4 Work as follows:

Rows 1 through 17 Work the stitches with 11°s (this was done for the beginning).

Row 18 Work the stitches with 11°s, adding one 15° at the top of each stitch.

Row 19 Work the stitches with 8°s, adding one 11° at the top of each stitch.

Row 20 Work the stitches with 6°s, adding one 11° at the top and one 15° at the bottom of each stitch.

Row 21 Work the stitches with 6°s, adding one 11° at the top and one 11° at the bottom of each stitch.

Row 22 Work the stitches with 8°s, adding one 15° at the top and one 11° at the bottom of each stitch.

SUPPLIES

Size 11° variegated blue-lined crystal round seed beads, 24 grams

Size 15° light sapphire/bronze-lined AB round seed beads, 2 grams

Size 8° candlelight matte silver-lined AB round seed beads, 6 grams

Size 6° matte transparent gray AB round seed beads, 22 grams

11 black round glass beads (druks), 8 mm

Size 12 beading needles

Beading thread

Beading mat

Scissors

FINISHED SIZE

19½ inches (49.5 cm) long, excluding clasp

TECHNIQUE

Herringbone stitch

Row 23 Work the stitches with 11°s, adding one 11° at the bottom of each stitch.

Row 24 Work the stitches with 11°s, adding one 15° at the bottom of each stitch; insert an 8-mm round bead.

5 Repeat Rows 1 through 24 until the rope is 2¼ inches (5.7 cm) shorter than your desired finished length.

6 Finish the rope with 17 rows of herringbone stitch using 11°s. Ladder stitch the herringbone columns together on the end.

▶ Make the Toggle Bar

Create a herringbone tube starting with six size 11° beads (three stitches). Work 13 rounds. Ladder stitch the ends of the tube together.

▶ Attach the Toggle Bar

With the thread exiting a bead on the end of the rope, string three 11°s, one 6°, and two more 11°s. Pass through a center bead on the toggle bar. String two 11°s, pass back down through the 6°, and string three 11°s. Weave back into the rope, passing through a bead on the opposite side of the rope end from where you started (figure 2). Reinforce this path two more times.

▶ Create the Loop

Exiting a bead on the opposite end of the rope, string three 11°s, one 6°, and enough 11°s to circle the toggle bar (I used 29 beads in my loop, but you may need to use slightly more or fewer depending on the size of your beads). Pass back through the 6°, and string three 11°s. Weave back into the rope, passing through a bead on the opposite side of the rope end from where you started (figure 3). On the second pass to reinforce the loop, pass through one 11°, and then peyote stitch around the loop. On the third and last pass to reinforce the loop, peyote stitch around with two 15°s in each stitch.

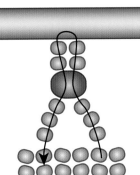

figure 2

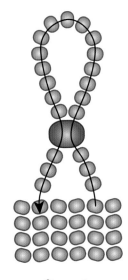

figure 3

VARIATION

FIGURE-EIGHT EARRINGS

The graceful curves of the figure-eight shape are embellished with sparkling tiny crystals and an elegant pearl teardrop to create an earring that you can wear with jeans and gowns alike.

SUPPLIES

Size 11° denim blue matte metallic iris round seed beads, 3 grams

26 light amethyst verde crystal rounds, 2 mm

2 bright gold teardrop pearls, 11 x 8 mm

2 gold-filled ear wires

Size 10 or 12 beading needles

Beading thread

Beading mat

Scissors

FINISHED SIZE

2½ inches (6.4 cm) long, excluding ear wire

TECHNIQUES

Herringbone stitch

Ladder stitch

▶ Bead Herringbone Rings

Create two lengths of tubular herringbone stitch rope with 11°s, two stitches around and 50 rows long. Join the ends together to form a ring. End the threads and set the two rings aside.

▶ Make the Crystal Wraps

1 Pick up one 11°, one crystal, two 11°s, one crystal, and one 11°. From the tail end moving upward, pass through the first three beads—the beads that were on top will fold over so that you'll have three beads next to three beads (figure 1). (You might have to nudge them a little so they fold over the way they should.)

2 Continue with ladder stitch, adding sets of one 11°, one crystal, and one 11° until you have a total of 13 sets.

figure 1

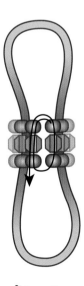

figure 2

3 Join the two ends together around a herringbone ring, cinching it into a figure eight (figure 2).

4 Repeat to make a second crystal wrap that cinches a herringbone ring into a figure-eight shape.

▶ Insert the Pearls

1 With the thread exiting one of the two 11°s at the bottom center of the herringbone rope, pick up one pearl and one 11°, and pass through two 11°s in the herringbone rope that is tucked behind the crystal wrap. You can wiggle the crystal wrap up and down a bit to get at the beads you need to pass through on the rope.

2 Reinforce this path several times. Center the pearl by passing through the two centered 11°s on the bottom of the second column of the herringbone rope, and attach it to the second side of the rope under the crystal wrap (figure 3).

3 Repeat for the other figure eight.

▶ Attach the Ear Wires

With the thread exiting one of the two 11°s at the top of a figure eight, pick up one 11°, pass through the ear wire, and pick up one 11°. Pass back through the two centered 11°s. Reinforce this path at least once more, then attach to the two centered 11°s on the second column of herringbone rope to center the ear wire over the rope (figure 4).

Repeat to hang the other figure eight from an ear wire.

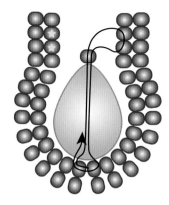

figure 3

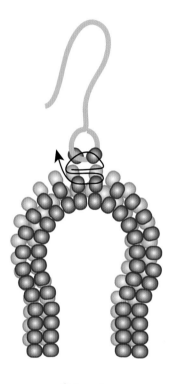

figure 4

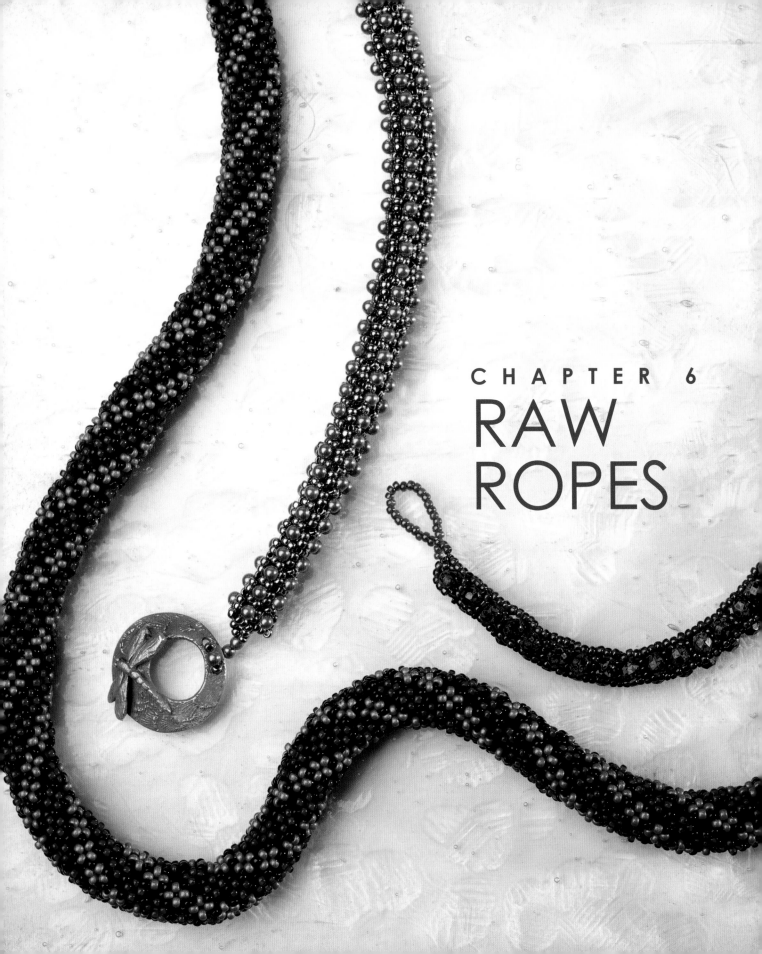

BOHEMIAN EARRINGS

An architecturally shaped tube of sparkling fire-polished
beads is finished off with lengths of dancing chain.
The motion and sway of these earrings are captivating.

SUPPLIES

72 teal Apollo Czech fire-polished
round beads, 3 mm

26 inches (66 cm) of small brass
rollo chain

2 brass ear wires

Size 10 or 12 beading needles

Beading thread

Beading mat

Scissors

Wire cutters

Needle-nose pliers

FINISHED SIZE

3 inches (7.6 cm) long,
excluding ear wire

TECHNIQUE

RAW

► Bead the Rope

1 Create a flat piece of RAW with one fire-polished bead per side that is four units wide by three units tall.

2 With the thread exiting one of the fire-polished beads on the long edge, join the two long edges to form a tube by completing a fourth RAW unit between the two (figure 1). Do not end the working thread (you may end off the tail thread) and set the tube aside.

3 Repeat to make a second RAW tube.

► Prepare the Chain

1 Cut 12 pieces of chain that are 1 inch (2.5 cm) long for each earring, 24 pieces total. Your chain may vary from the sample, but that worked out to be 20 links per inch (2.5 cm).

2 Cut two pieces of chain that are ⅝ inch (1.6 cm) long (seven links in the sample) for each earring, four pieces total.

Tip: Here's an easy way to cut chain the same length without having to count links each time. Count the links on the first piece of chain and cut it—no way around that one! Hang that piece of chain from the last link on a piece of wire or an awl. Now hang the last link of the bulk length of chain next to it. Hold it up and you'll see where the short length of chain hangs next to the long length, and you'll be able to cut the correct link.

► Attach the Chains

1 With the thread exiting a fire-polished bead on one end of the tube, pick up the end link on a 1-inch (2.5 cm) piece of chain and pass through the next fire-polished bead straight ahead (figure 2). Work your way around the bottom layer of fire-polished beads, adding a length of chain at each intersection (four lengths total). Reinforce the entire layer one more time.

2 Repeat on the next two layers of fire-polished beads. If you hold the chains in your nondominant hand while you stitch, it will help keep them from tangling with the thread.

3 Work your way to the top layer of fire-polished beads. Pick up one of the smaller pieces of chain and pass through the next fire-polished bead. Work your way over to the intersection that is diagonally opposite from where you added the chain and add the second small piece of chain.

4 Attach the ends of two chains on the top to the ear wire.

5 Repeat the steps to make a second earring.

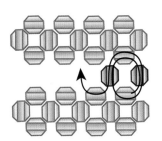

figure 1

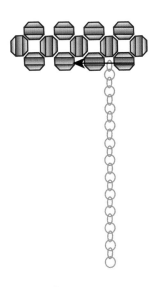

figure 2

HEIRLOOM NECKLACE

This necklace comprises two separate ropes that are joined together at the ends. The outer rope combines netting and right angle weave, which creates a beautiful pattern; however, without an inner support, the rope collapses flat. The inner rope is a simple peyote-stitched form that, when inserted inside the outer rope, provides a framework that keeps the necklace rounded.

▶ Bead the Outer Rope

Row 1 Using a comfortable length of thread, string 18 beads as follows: B, A, A, C, A, A, B, A, A, C, A, A, B, A, A, C, A, A. Pass through all the beads again to form a ring, and then pass through the first four beads again so you're exiting the first C bead. Pick up three Cs and pass again through the C bead in the ring, creating a RAW unit. Pass forward through three beads in the ring so you're exiting a B bead. Create another RAW unit on top of the B bead by picking up three Bs and passing again through the B in the ring. Continue adding RAW units on top of the B and C beads, using their respective colors, until you've completed five RAW units on the ring (figure 1).

Adding Rows Exit the remaining B and pick up one A and four Bs. Pass again through the first B, creating a RAW unit. If necessary, pinch the bottom B bead and move the RAW unit so it's snugged up against the rest of the beadwork and no extra thread is showing. (I usually have to do this with every stitch, but tight beaders may not have the same issue.) Pick up one A and pass through the outer tip bead of the next RAW unit in the ring (figure 2).

To help hold the tension, reinforce the RAW unit your thread is exiting by passing through all four beads in the unit (figure 3). Repeat these steps: pick up one A, four beads of the appropriate color, make a RAW unit, and pick up one A; pass through the tip of the next RAW unit, and then reinforce the RAW unit on the previous row, until the rope is the desired length. The color of the RAW unit you're adding will match the color of the bead you're exiting.

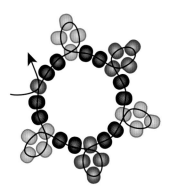

figure 1

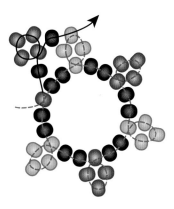

figure 2

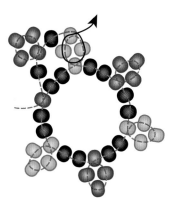

figure 3

SUPPLIES

Size 11° round seed beads

    Color A: black, 14 grams

    Color B: amber/dark cranberry lined, 14 grams

    Color C: rose copper matte permanent galvanized, 14 grams

Size 8° black round seed beads, 30 grams

Raku donut, 32 mm

Size 10 or 12 beading needles

Beading thread

Beading mat

Scissors

Large-eye needle, 5 inches (12.7 cm) long

FINISHED SIZE

20¼ inches (51.5 cm) long, excluding clasp

TECHNIQUES

Netting without step up

RAW

Peyote stitch

▶ Bead the Inner Rope

When you've reached the desired length, you'll need to make an inner rope and insert it into the outer rope, then work the final rows to finish off the ends. Make a circular-peyote-stitch rope of size 8° beads, starting with an eight-bead ring. The inner rope should be just shy of the length of the outer rope. End your threads.

▶ Insert the Inner Rope

Cut a piece of thread about 24 inches (61 cm) long and thread it onto a long large-eye needle. Poke the needle and thread through the middle of the inner rope, about two rows down from the end. Center the thread and put the other thread end through the needle also. Use the needle to guide the inner rope down the center of the outer rope. Feed the needle through as far as the thread will allow, and then pull on the thread and wiggle the outer rope to help the inner rope move

forward. I find that you can work the outer rope along like an inchworm, moving it over the inner rope. Keep feeding the inner rope along until it touches the last row of the outer rope. Make one last adjustment by holding the two ropes up and smoothing the outer rope down to make sure it's fully extended. If necessary, you can make adjustments to the length of the inner rope at this time by adding or removing rows.

▶ Tack the Ropes Together

Attach a new thread to one end of the outer rope, pass through the inner rope, pass through a few beads in the outer rope, and then pass through the inner rope again to reach the opposite side of the outer rope. Repeat four or five times until it feels secure. Now weave your thread to the edge of the outer rope and follow the Bead the Final Rows instructions to the right. Repeat this step at the other end of the rope.

TIP

You may find it helpful to work over a dowel, though I don't. I find it works best to hold the rope sideways. Experiment with different positions to find what works for you. Watch for caught threads as you're going along.

▶ Bead the Final Rows

Now that the ropes are joined, you'll taper and close up the ends, making them ready for the clasp. You'll use one method to close the finishing end of the rope and another for the starting end.

Taper the Starting End

Start a new thread that exits a B or C bead. Pick up one 8° and pass through the next C or B in the ring. Repeat to add a total of six beads. Exiting the first 8° added, peyote stitch around with 8° beads, stepping up at the end of the row. Peyote stitch around with A beads and step up. Decrease by making one A peyote stitch, then skipping the next space; repeat this around, adding a total of three As. Reinforce the three As and pull inward to tighten and center them.

Taper the Finishing End

With the thread exiting a B or C tip bead, pick up two As and pass through the next B or C tip bead; repeat, adding two As between all the tip beads in the row. Then follow the directions for Taper the Starting End above to finish the rope (figure 4).

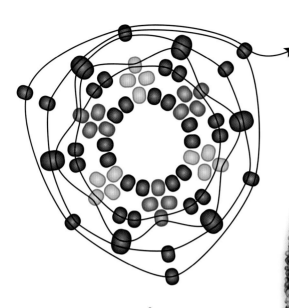

figure 4

▶ Attach the Donut

Exiting one of the three beads in the last row of one end of the outer rope, pick up enough As to make a loop that will comfortably fit through the donut and back to the rope. I used 30—you may need to use slightly more or fewer depending on the size of your beads. Pass through the same bead in the outer rope. Pass through the next bead of the last row and make a second loop of As. Pass through the same bead you exited from. Reinforce both of these loops at least one more time, and then end off your thread.

▶ Make the Toggle Bar

Using As, make a peyote-stitch strip that is 10 beads wide and 10 beads long. Fold the strip lengthwise and zip the sides together. Drop the needle down the center of the tube (to center the outside embellishment) and pick up one 8° and one B or C (your choice). Pass back through the 8° and through the center of the tube. Pick up one 8° and one B or C, then pass back through the 8° and through the center of the tube. Reinforce this path twice more, and then end off the thread in the tube.

▶ Attach the Toggle Bar

Exiting one of the three beads in the last row of the other end of the outer rope, pick up five As and pass through two beads diagonally at the center side of the toggle bar. Pick up five more As and pass through the bead you exited in the outer rope. Pass through the next bead in the outer rope, pick up five As, then pass through the same two beads as before in the side of the toggle bar. Pick up five As and pass through the same bead in the outer rope. Reinforce both lines of attachment one more time, then end off your thread.

LADIES
WHO
LUNCH
NECKLACE

The traditional pearl necklace gets an upgrade to modern in this beauty. The magic of multiples creates a fresh take that is sure to grab attention.

▶ Make the Rope

1 Start by making a flat piece of RAW with 11°s that uses two beads on each side of the units and is four rows wide by the length you desire.

2 Connect the long edges together by completing a fifth RAW unit between the two, forming a tube (figure 1).

▶ Embellish the Rope

With the thread exiting a RAW corner bead, pick up a pearl and pass through the two beads diagonally opposite the exited corner bead (figure 2). Repeat until all the RAW units are filled with pearls.

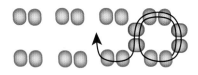

figure 1

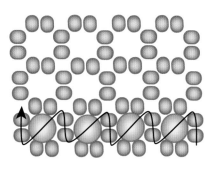

figure 2

SUPPLIES

Size 11° brass gold iris round seed beads, 20 grams

490 copper crystal pearls, 3 mm

Bronze toggle clasp, 1 inch (2.5 cm) in diameter

Size 10 or 12 beading needles

Beading thread

Beading mat

Scissors

FINISHED SIZE

18 inches (45.7 cm) long, excluding clasp

TECHNIQUE

RAW

▶ Finish the Ends

With the thread exiting the outside edge of a RAW unit, pick up one 11° and pass through the two 11°s of the next RAW unit (figure 3). Repeat until you have gone around the rope end, and then do the same on the other side of the rope.

▶ Attach the Clasp

Choose three point beads equidistant apart on one end of the rope. Exiting the first point bead, pick up two 11°s, two pearls, three 11°s, one half of the clasp, and then three 11°s; pass back through the two pearls, pick up two 11°s, and pass through the next point bead in the rope edge. Move along the edge until you're exiting the third point bead, pick up two 11°s, and pass through the two pearls. Reinforce each leg of the tripod, if possible. Repeat on the other side with the other half of the clasp.

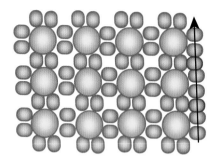

figure 3

92

REFLECTIONS BRACELET

Surprisingly, the base of this versatile bracelet is a triangle-shaped tube of faceted

fire-polished beads. You could substitute crystal bicones for even more sparkle and shine.

SUPPLIES

Size 11° Montana/emerald-lined round seed beads, 4 grams

62 Picasso jet Czech fire-polished round beads, 4 mm

30 size 15° black round seed beads

Size 12 beading needles

Beading thread

Beading mat

Scissors

FINISHED SIZE

8 inches (20.3 cm) long, including clasp

TECHNIQUES

RAW

Peyote stitch

▶ Bead the Rope

1 Create a flat strip of RAW that uses three 11°s per side and is two units wide by the length you desire.

2 You'll now join the outside edges of the strip, forming a triangular tube by making a third row between them. With the thread exiting a set of three 11°s at the end of one long side, string three 11°s; fold the two rows of the strip into a V shape, and then pass through the corresponding three 11°s on the other side. String three 11°s and pass though the next three 11°s on the side originally exited (figure 1). Continue until you have joined the two sides along the entire length of the strip.

▶ Embellish the Rope

1 Holding the RAW tube horizontally, weave through the beadwork so the thread exits the first three 11°s on one end from top to bottom. Pick up one fire-polished bead and pass through the three 11°s on the opposite side of the RAW unit from top to bottom (figure 2).

2 When you've reached the end of the row, turn the bracelet and repeat to add embellishment on one other side of the triangle, working in the opposite direction from the first row.

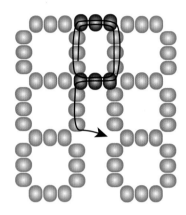

figure 1

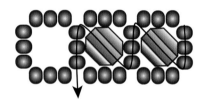

figure 2

Underside

3 With the thread exiting the first three 11°s along the top edge of the tube between the rows of fire-polished beads, pick up one 15° and pass through the next three 11°s (figure 3). Repeat along the entire length. Don't pull too tightly—this step is just to add a decorative and finishing touch. If you pull too hard, you'll curve the tube.

▶ Bead the Clasp

1 Create a toggle bar with 11°s by making a peyote-stitch strip beginning with 10 beads for rows 1 and 2, and beading a total of 10 rows. Zip the last row to the first to create a tube.

2 With the thread exiting the three 11°s on the bottom outside edge of the unembellished side, string five 11°s and pass through two center beads on a diagonal in the peyote toggle bar. Pick up two 11°s and pass back through the third of the five 11°s previously added, and then pick up two more 11°s and pass through the original three 11°s on the rope (figure 4). Reinforce this pathway at least two more times.

3 On the other end of the rope, weave through the beadwork so the thread exits the corresponding three 11°s and string enough 11°s to circle the toggle bar; I used 24—you may need to use slightly more or fewer depending on the size of your beads. Pass back through the third 11° added, pick up two more 11°s, and pass through the original three 11°s on the rope (figure 5). Reinforce this pathway at least two more times.

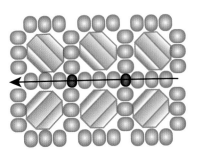

figure 3

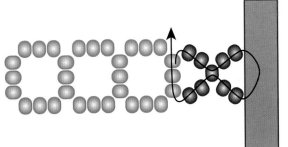

figure 4

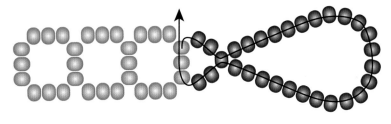

figure 5

CHAPTER 7
OTHER STITCHES

BUTTERFLY KISSES NECKLACE

The Oglala stitch is also commonly known as the butterfly stitch and is traditionally a delicate, ethereal wave of beads. Here I've created a more substantial rope, stacking several passes of the stitch together to create a richer and more ample appearance.

▶ Bead the Base Row

1 String the end of the wire through a crimp bead, through the loop of one half of the clasp, and back through the crimp bead. Leaving about a 1-inch (2.5 cm) overlap of beading wire, use needle-nose pliers to flatten the crimp bead, or use crimping pliers for a folded crimp if you prefer.

2 String five 6°s, then a length of 8°s equal to the length of necklace you desire; string another five 6°s.

3 Attach the other end of the clasp as in step 1, leaving about two beads' worth of extra slack in the necklace length as you crimp. Tuck the overlapping beading wire down through the end beads.

Note: You will only need to use size 6° beads on the ends when using a coated seed bead like the permanent galvanized beads. The coating makes the hole smaller, which can be problematic given the number of passes of beading wire and thread that will need to fit through the hole.

4 To attach the thread, pass through three beads 1 inch (2.5 cm) or so from the clasp, moving toward the clasp. Tie a surgeon's knot around the beading wire, and then work forward through another few beads. Make another knot. Make at least three knots as you work the thread so it exits between the first two seed beads next to the crimp bead (figure 1, next page).

Note: Because the crimp bead can cut the thread over time, leave one seed bead as a buffer between the crimp and the thread.

SUPPLIES

Size 6° permanent galvanized gold round seed beads, 1 gram

Size 8° permanent galvanized gold round seed beads, 9 grams

Size 11° permanent galvanized gold round seed beads, 60 grams

120 gold crystal bicones, 4 mm

2 gold crimps beads

.014- or .015-diameter beading wire, 25 inches (63.5 cm)

Square brass clasp, ¾ inch (1.9 cm) across

Size 12 beading needles

Beading thread

Beading mat

Scissors

Wire cutters

Needle-nose pliers or crimping pliers

FINISHED SIZE

19½ inches (49.5 cm) long, excluding clasp

TECHNIQUE

Oglala stitch

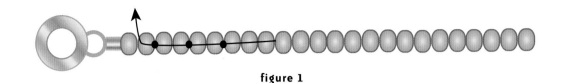

figure 1

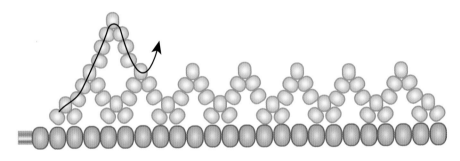

figure 2

▶ Add the First Wave

1 String three 11°s, skip two beads on the base, and pass through the next bead (figure 2). Repeat along the entire length of the base row.

Note: If the number of beads on your base doesn't come out exactly right, don't stress about it. You can skip three seed beads on the base if necessary, or skip only one. The important thing is to finish by exiting between the last two seed beads, the way you did on the other end.

2 Tie a knot around the base so you can turn and work in the opposite direction. Pass through the first two 11°s of the first wave; *string five 11°s and then pass through the middle 11° of the next wave (figure 3). Repeat from * along the entire length.

3 Tie a knot and turn again; weave through the beadwork so the thread exits the middle 11° of the wave of five. *String seven 11°s and pass through the middle 11° of the next wave (figure 4). Repeat from * along the entire length.

▶ Add the Second Wave

With the thread exiting the third bead from the end on the base, repeat the steps of the first wave. Staggering the start of this pass will give a full, rounded look to your rope (figure 5).

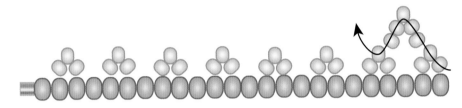

figure 3

figure 4

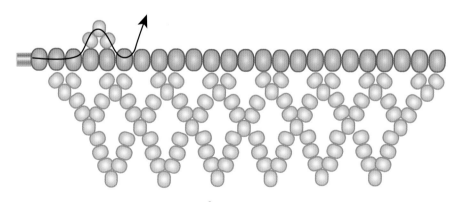

figure 5

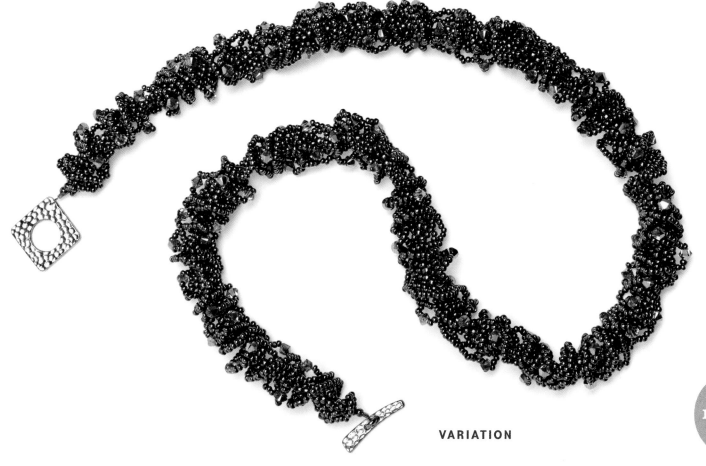

VARIATION

▶ Add the Third Wave

With the thread exiting the second bead from the end on the base, repeat steps 1 and 2 of the first wave. On step 3, instead of stringing seven 11°s, string three 11°s, one crystal, and three 11°s.

▶ Options

• Add a focal bead in the middle on your base row—when you get to that spot when adding the waves, simply pass through the focal bead to get to the other side and keep adding waves.

• Add focal beads throughout the neck-lace—you can evenly space larger focal beads to peek out from the waves on the base row.

• Can you make it with all size 8° seed beads? Of course you can! It will be quicker because the scale will be larger. It does make for a significantly heavier necklace, though, so be sure to take that into account.

• Make it with a bead color mixture to create a color riot!

• Try making each pass of waves (the 3s, the 5s, and the 7s) a different color to create an ombré design.

FINDING BALANCE
BRACELET

A traditional way of making a bracelet with peyote tube spacers is to create all the pieces separately and assemble them at the end. That's not how this one is made, though. Instead, the spacer beads are built off the base rope. Kind of a cool trick, if I do say so myself!

▶ Bead the Base Rope

1 Make a flat piece with peyote stitch using 10 As for the first row, and making it 10 rows long. Zip the last row to the first row to form a tube.

2 Weave through the beadwork so the thread exits one of the outside edge As. Begin working brick stitch by picking up two As, passing your needle under the thread attaching the A you're exiting and the A next to it, and then passing back up through the second A added (figure 1).

3 Pick up one A and pass the needle under the next thread and back up through the A just added. Continue around to add a total of five As. After adding the last bead, pass down through the first A and up through the last A to connect them (figure 2).

4 Repeat steps 2 and 3 until your rope is the desired length.

figure 1

figure 2

SUPPLIES

Size 11° round seed beads

 Color A: green teal matte metallic iris, 6.5 grams

 Color B: olivine-lined AB, 6.5 grams

 Color C: opaque bright turquoise, 1 gram

Glass button, approximately ¾ inch (19 mm) in diameter

Size 12 beading needles

Beading thread

Beading mat

Scissors

FINISHED SIZE

Approximately 8 inches (20.3 cm) long, excluding clasp

TECHNIQUES

Peyote stitch

Brick stitch

▶ Attach the Embellishments

1 Weave through the beadwork from the outside edge into the rope until the thread exits a bead in the tenth row down. Pick up one B and stitch in the ditch (figure 3). Continue in this manner until you have a total of six beads. Work peyote stitch with Bs off the six beads to make a flat piece that is 22 rows long.

2 Zip the flat piece of peyote around the base rope to the original six Bs.

3 With the thread exiting one of the outside edge Bs, pick up one C and pass down through the next B. Pass up through the next B on the edge, and pick up one C (figure 4). Continue adding Cs along the edge, going around twice to fill in all the spots. Repeat on the other side of the tube embellishment.

4 Repeat steps 1 through 3 to add four more embellished tubes along the base rope, spacing them about ½ inch (1.3 cm) apart. I like to count 10 rows of base beads (including the rows under the embellishment) to make sure they are spaced evenly. You can make size adjustments

as necessary by changing the number of rows between the peyote tubes or by adding or removing rows at the clasp ends of the base rope.

figure 3

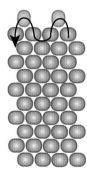

figure 4

▶ Attach the Clasp

1 With the thread exiting one of the outside edge As, pick up two As, the button, and two more As. Pass through an A on the opposite side of the outside edge. Reinforce this path at least twice more.

2 For the loop end of the clasp, weave through the beadwork so the thread exits one of the outside edge As; string two As, one B, and 40 As; pass back through the B, pick up two more As, and then pass through an A on the opposite side of the outside edge. When you reinforce this path, peyote stitch around the loop with As on the second pass. On the third pass, peyote stitch around the loop, alternating two Bs with one B.

REVELATIONS BRACELET

The soft tube of this bracelet can flatten against your wrist and be worn to show different color options.

Show a side with all one color, all the other color, or mix it up with one row of each visible!

SUPPLIES

Size 11° steel blue luster round seed beads, 4.5 grams

3-mm Czech fire-polished beads

   Color A: copper-lined crystal, 130

   Color B: Apollo sapphire, 126

Size 10 beading needles

Beading thread

Beading mat

Scissors

FINISHED SIZE

8 inches (20.3 cm) long, excluding clasp

TECHNIQUES

Chevron stitch

Peyote stitch

▶ Bead the Chevron Stitch Rope

Row 1 String five 11°s, one A, one 11°, and one A; pass back through all the beads again to form a ring, leaving about a 6-inch (15.2 cm) tail at the start. With the thread exiting the 11° between the two As, string four 11°s and one A; pass back through the last 11° in the previous group of five (figure 1). *String four 11°s and one A; pass back through the 11° on the other side of the A previously added. Repeat from * until you have the desired length (sample has 63 beads along each side).

Tip: I like to flip my work with each new row so I'm always working in the same direction.

Row 2 With the thread exiting an 11° on the bottom, pick up one 11°, one A, five 11°s, and one A, then pass back through the first 11° picked up (figure 2). Pass through the three 11°s across the bottom of the previous row, then *pick up one 11° and one A; pass through the first 11° past the previously added A (figure 3). String four 11°s and one A and pass back through

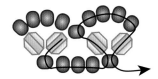

figure 1

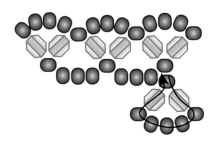

figure 2

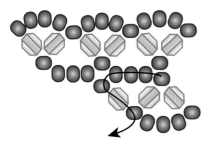

figure 3

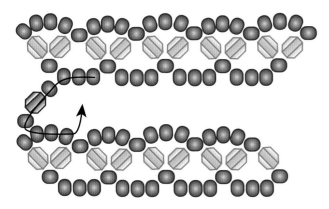

figure 4

figure 5

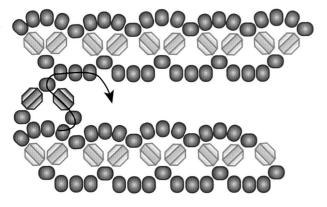

figure 6

the first 11° past the previously added A in the "corner" and then pass through the three 11°s along the bottom of the previous row (figure 4). Repeat from * along the entire length of the bracelet.

Row 3 Repeat Row 2, but use B instead of A.

Row 4 On this row, you'll join the edges of the flat chevron rows together to create a rope. With the thread exiting one of the three beads along the bottom edge toward the outside, pick up one 11°, one B, and one 11°. Folding your beadwork so the long sides are perpendicular, pass through the three edge beads along the opposite side (figure 5). *Pick up one 11° and one B and pass back through the first 11° added in the previous step, then through the next three 11°s along the opposite edge (figure 6). Repeat from * along the entire length of the bracelet.

Continued on next page

▶ Bead the Clasp

1 Create a tube toggle bar with 11°s by making a flat peyote-stitch piece that is 10 beads wide by 10 rows long. Zip the last row to the first row to form a tube. Add embellishment on the toggle bar ends with one A topped by an 11° on each side.

2 With the thread exiting the last 11° between two fire-polished beads, string three 11°s, one A, and two 11°s and pass through two center 11°s in the toggle bar. Pick up two 11°s and pass back through the A bead, and then pick up two more 11°s. (I like to add three beads on the indented side and only two beads on the pronounced side to even out my clasp.) Pass back through the 11°, A, and 11° on the edge (figure 7). Reinforce this path at least twice more.

3 With the thread exiting the last 11° between two fire-polished beads on the other end, string three 11°s, one A, and enough 11°s to loop around the toggle bar. (I used 28 in the sample). Pass back through the A, and then pick up two more 11°s and pass through the 11°, A, and 11° on the edge (figure 8). On the first reinforcement pass, peyote stitch around the loop, ending two beads shy of the A. On the last reinforcement pass, peyote stitch around the loop with two beads in each stitch.

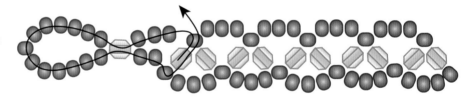

figure 7

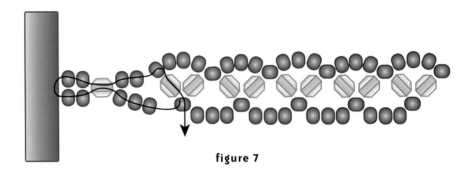

figure 8

BONNIE VIGIL

Open Lace Rope, 2010

24 x 17 x 1 cm

Seed beads, crystals

PHOTO BY CHRIS ROUDABUSH

JEROME NUÑEZ

Cascading Crystals, 2010

Rope, 43.2 cm long

Seed beads, crystal bicones;
Russian leaves, spiral rope

PHOTO BY CHRIS ROUDABUSH

NANCY DALE

Horn of Ammon, 2011

45.7 cm long

Cylinder beads, seed beads, crystal stones,
crystal beads, ammonite cabochon, freshwater
pearls, button; RAW, netting, peyote stitch,
bead embroidery

PHOTO BY SHERWOOD LAKE PHOTOGRAPHY

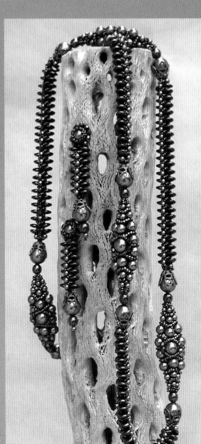

CAROL-ANNE WILSON

Réaltaí (Stars), **2011**

104.1 cm long, including fringe

Seed beads, cylinder beads, vintage chatons, crystal rivolis, bicones, drop bead; no-step netting, peyote stitch, herringbone stitch, embellished

PHOTO BY DAVID WILSON

TOP RIGHT

MELANIE POTTER

Segmentations, **2011**

40 x 25 x 2 cm

Seed beads, freshwater pearls, crystals; chevron chain

PHOTO BY SCOTT POTTER

BOTTOM

MIKKI FERRUGIARO

Spinal Tap Rope and Earrings, **2011**

Rope, 101 x 2 x 1.5 cm; earrings, each 6.5 x 1.5 x 1.5 cm

Seed beads, glass pearls, lentils, fire-polished glass beads, brass filigree; RAW, embellished

PHOTO BY ARTIST

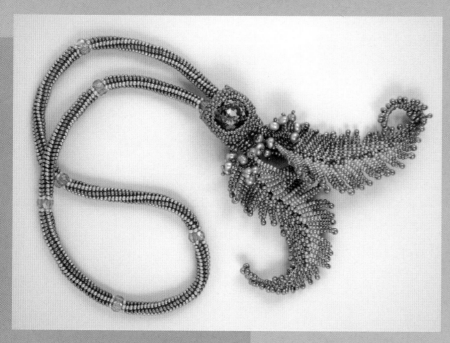

TOP

MELISSA GRAKOWSKY

Fern Lariat, 2010

25 x 8 x 2 cm

Seed beads, crystals, pearls, glass beads; herringbone stitch, peyote stitch

PHOTO BY ARTIST

BOTTOM RIGHT

MELISSA GRAKOWSKY

Cosmic Knots, 2011

25 x 8 x 1 cm

Pyrite, seed beads; netting

PHOTO BY ARTIST

LEFT

MELISSA GRAKOWSKY

Inexplicably Ndebele, 2009

25 x 8 x 1 cm

Crystal beads, seed beads, fire-polished beads; herringbone stitch

PHOTO BY ARTIST

TOP LEFT

NANCY CAIN

Cain's Chain, **2007**

Rope, 1 cm wide

Seed beads, crystal bicones; peyote stitch, rope

PHOTO BY DAVE WOLVERTON

TOP RIGHT

NANCY CAIN

Cain's Chain, **2007**

Rope, 1 cm wide

Seed beads, crystal bicones; peyote stitch, rope

PHOTO BY DAVE WOLVERTON

BOTTOM

NANCY CAIN

Serendipity, **2003**

Rope, 1.5 cm wide

Seed beads; netting

PHOTO BY DAVE WOLVERTON

TOP LEFT

CAROL-ANNE WILSON

Caora (Berries), **2011**

106.7 cm long

Seed beads, bugle beads, glass pearls, pearls, crystal rivolis and bicones; no-step netting, peyote stitch, herringbone stitch, netting, embellished

PHOTO BY DAVID WILSON

TOP RIGHT

NANCY DALE

Color Play Version #2, **2011**

152.4 cm long

Seed beads, turquoise, copper beads; cubic RAW variation

PHOTO BY SHERWOOD LAKE PHOTOGRAPHY

BOTTOM

NANCY CAIN

Cain's Chain (Big Version), **2007**

Rope, 1.5 cm wide

Seed beads, bicone crystals, lampwork beads; peyote stitch, new stitch

PHOTO BY DAVE WOLVERTON

TOP LEFT

JILL WISEMAN

Free Floating, 2009

58.4 cm long

Seed beads, crystals, magnetic clasp, lampwork glass pendant; spiral herringbone stitch, peyote stitch

PHOTO BY DAVID ORR

BOTTOM LEFT

JILL WISEMAN

Curly-Q, 2009

25.4 cm long

Seed beads; peyote stitch

PHOTO BY DAVID ORR

BOTTOM RIGHT

JILL WISEMAN

Dazzling Dutch Spiral, 2009

20.3 cm long

Seed beads, crystals, magnetic clasp; Dutch spiral

PHOTO BY DAVID ORR

TOP LEFT

JILL WISEMAN

Russian Splendor, 2008

61 cm long, including leaves

Seed beads, fire-polished glass beads; netting, peyote stitch

PHOTO BY DAVID ORR

TOP RIGHT

JILL WISEMAN

Sparkling Twining Vine Lariat, 2011

127 cm long

Seed beads, crystals; herringbone stitch, fringing

PHOTO BY DAVID ORR

BOTTOM

JILL WISEMAN

Fish Lariat, 2010

137.2 cm long

Seed beads, glass lampwork bead; double spiral rope, fringing

PHOTO BY DAVID ORR

JILL WISEMAN AND MICK MCNULTY

Wacky Pearls, 2009

50.8 cm long, 2.5 cm wide

Freshwater pearls, seed beads,
toggle clasp; netting

PHOTO BY DAVID ORR

ABOVE

JILL WISEMAN

Shell Game, 2011

50.8 cm long

Seed beads, bugle beads,
toggle clasp; spiral rope

PHOTO BY DAVID ORR

LEFT

JILL WISEMAN

Rolling, 2009

55.9 cm long

Seed beads, glass button;
double spiral rope

PHOTO BY DAVID ORR

JILL WISEMAN

Dolly, 2011

66 cm long, including pendant bead

Seed beads, crystals, lampwork glass bead;
double spiral rope, peyote stitch

PHOTO BY DAVID ORR

117

ABOUT THE AUTHOR

Photo by Korey Howell

Jill Wiseman stumbled across the world of beads in 2001, and since then her life hasn't been the same. Her early exploration into all areas of jewelry making and design quickly narrowed to one true love—beadweaving. Her natural aptitude for the craft was encouraged by local instructors and eventually led to a full-time teaching and design career of her own, first locally and now nationwide. Jill has taught at the Bead&Button Show, various Bead Fest shows, and bead stores and bead societies from coast to coast. She is known for her easygoing, vibrant personality in class, creating a stress-free and entertaining environment in which to learn new skills.

In addition to offering classes, Jill has partnered with her mother, June Wiseman, to create a business called Tapestry Beads. Their line of beadweaving kits and instructions for beaders of all experience levels is available at www.tapestrybeads.com. Jill and June live in Texas in a home filled with beady goodness and projects. Spoiled-rotten dogs Maggie and Winston and pampered cats Josie and Piper round out the never-dull household. Keep up with Jill on her blog at tapestrybeads.blogspot.com.

ACKNOWLEDGMENTS

I'm exceedingly lucky that my mother, June Wiseman, is not only my best friend, but she also shares this crazy passion for beadweaving and is my work partner, too. She has supported me financially and emotionally as we figured it all out and has lived through everything from the sad days of "I'm going to need to get a real job" to the panicked days of "I'm going to need to hire help!" I quite literally couldn't have gotten here without her. And yes, Mom, I know you spent 26 hours in labor with me!

My brother and sister-in-law, Rich and Becky, have been generous in their encouragement, support, and willingness to listen to endless bead-related conversations at family dinners.

Heartfelt and tender thanks go to my first beadweaving teachers: Pam Way, Theresa Buchle, and elif ogan. You ladies introduced me to a magical world of tiny glass beads, needle, and thread that will captivate me for the rest of my life. I am eternally grateful.

Thanks to Norma, who pushed me to take the leap from office worker to full-time bead artist.

I'm grateful to the local ladies who have been my first students, my test beaders for new projects, and my friends. In particular, Kathryn Duckett was in the first class I ever took, and the second, and the third … She was a student in the first class I ever taught, and 10 years later, she's part of my family.

A book like this doesn't appear without a tribe of dedicated people making it happen:

My deepest thanks go to Andrew Thornton, who played matchmaker.

The endlessly patient Nathalie Mornu has been a dream editor, holding my hand, educating me about the process, and playing cheerleader along the way.

Judith Durant's technical editing makes me sound smart and has elevated my direction-writing skills to a new level.

Thanks to Ray Hemachandra for believing in me. You don't know it, but I burst into tears when I was first told this book would be part of the Beadweaving Master Class series. I'm so proud to stand among the other fine bead artists who came before me.

It's a good day when you discover that someone as talented as Melissa Grakowsky Shippee will be drawing your illustrations. Thanks for reading my mind!

Thanks to photographer Lynne Harty and model Colette Johnson for making my jewelry shine. The owners of Frock Boutique in Asheville helped, too, by loaning us some of their lovely garments for our photo shoot.

Finally, and very importantly, thank you so much to every single student and beader I have encountered over the years. You've kept me going with your enthusiasm and giggles and excitement. My job is a true joy because I get to spend time with you. This book is a love letter that I wrote just for you.

INDEX

STITCH INDEX

THE ESSENTIAL LIBRARY OF BOOKS FOR BEADERS

Diane Fitzgerald

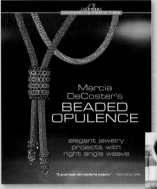

Marcia DeCoster

Laura McCabe

Sherry Serafini

Maggie Meister

Rachel Nelson-Smith

Sonoko Nozue

Sabine Lippert

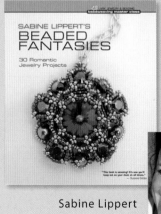

Jill Wiseman

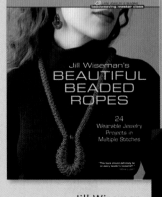

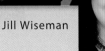